# APERTURE



Photographs by
Abbas, Constantino Arias, Lázaro Blanco, Agustín Víctor Casasola, Hugo Cifuentes, Laura Cohen, Raúl Corrales, Rafael Doniz, Víctor Flores Olea, Eduardo Frías, Héctor García, Graciela Iturbide, Elías Jaber, Eduardo Longoni, Nacho López, Agustín Martínez Castro, Pedro Meyer, Tina Modotti, Daniel Muzio, José Luis Neyra, Pablo Ortiz Monasterio, Rubén Ortiz Torres, Rodolfo del Percio, Josep Renau, Jorge Manuel Rilo, Miguel Rio Branco, and Mariana Yampolsky

# Río de Luz

*Aperture* has often focused on the work of individual photographers and countries but has rarely addressed the cross-cultural sensibilities of a particular region. "Río de Luz," or River of light, attempts to do just that. The title serves not only as a metaphor for the publication as a whole, but also for the fluidity with which its artists and images cross borders of all kinds. By moving through various experiences and issues common to many Latin American countries, "Río de Luz" celebrates a broad and diverse culture and its artists both in terms of what binds them and what distinguishes them from one another.

A tribute to the Mexican book series Río de Luz, one of the most important collections of Latin American photography ever compiled, this issue of *Aperture* was guest edited by Pablo Ortiz Monasterio, one of the original editors of the series. It affords our readers the unprecedented opportunity to experience the essence of this seminal, often controversial, short-lived series of books. At the same time, it reconsiders both the work and the themes embodied in the original books, offering insightful readings that intensify our understanding of the work. We are grateful for the intelligent and creative collaboration of all the writers and photographers, and of course to our esteemed friend and colleague, Pablo Ortiz Monasterio, who below introduces the project.

—The Editors

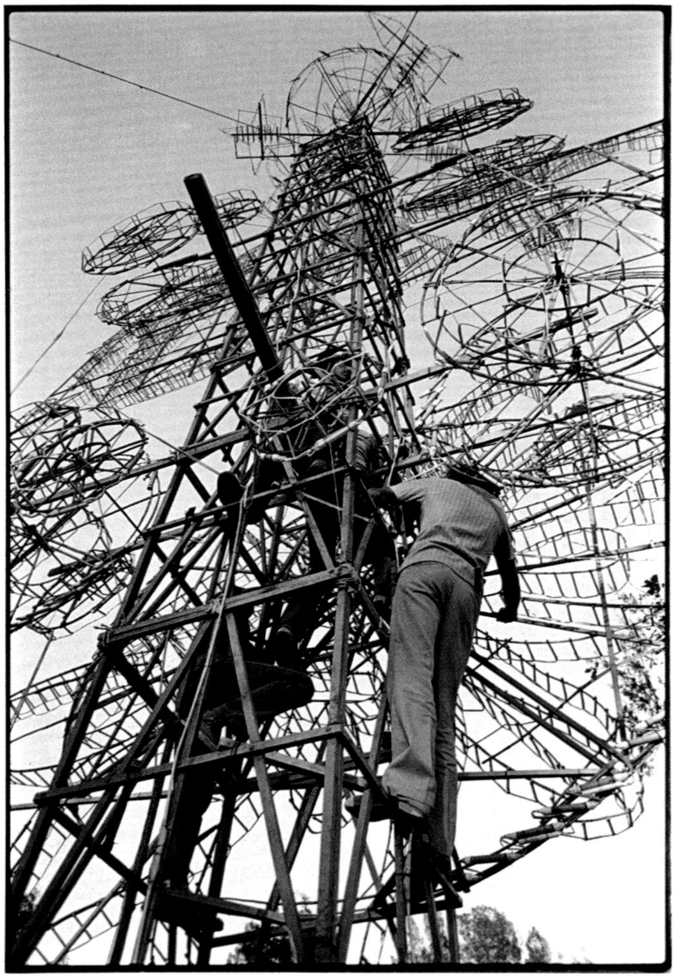

Víctor Flores Olea, *Castillo* (Fireworks), Mexico City, Mexico, 1982

Río de Luz began in 1984, and by 1989 twenty volumes had been published. The title, from a poem by Gilberto Owen, faithfully expresses the objectives which served as the driving force behind the project.

When Aperture proposed that we collaborate on an issue devoted to Río de Luz that, rather than be a "greatest hits" of the original series, would instead provide a new context for looking at the work ten to fifteen years later, I asked: how could we bring together the richness and complexity of the twenty volumes produced over the course of five years in this single issue—with the medley of topics covered and such magnificent photographic styles?

Our goal, then, was to incorporate as many images and photographers as possible, while revisiting the work from a contemporary perspective, and in light of changes in the cultural, political, and social climate of Latin America.

This volume opens with images from Mariana Yampolsky's *La raíz y el camino*, which reveals the subtleties of human relationships and the weight of tradition, together with some photographs from Lázaro Blanco's *Luces y tiempos*, in which his concise, rigorous compositions are outstanding. The text by Víctor Flores Olea, the multifaceted writer and the photographic author of one of the collection's volumes, gives an account of the origins and aspirations of Río de Luz.

The history of humanity has been built from wars and revolutions. The second chapter covers some of those taking place in Latin America during this century. The text written by art critic and historian Raquel Tibol contextualizes the compelling photographs of the Mexican Revolution at the beginning of the century, which were published in the book *Jefes, héroes y caudillos* from the Casasola Archive; images from the war that overthrew Nicaragua's tyrannical Somoza in the late 1970s, which were captured in Pedro Meyer's *Espejo de espinas*; and the powerful images from the last period of Argentina's military dictatorship, which were portrayed by an extensive group of local photojournalists and brought together in the book *Democracia vigilada*.

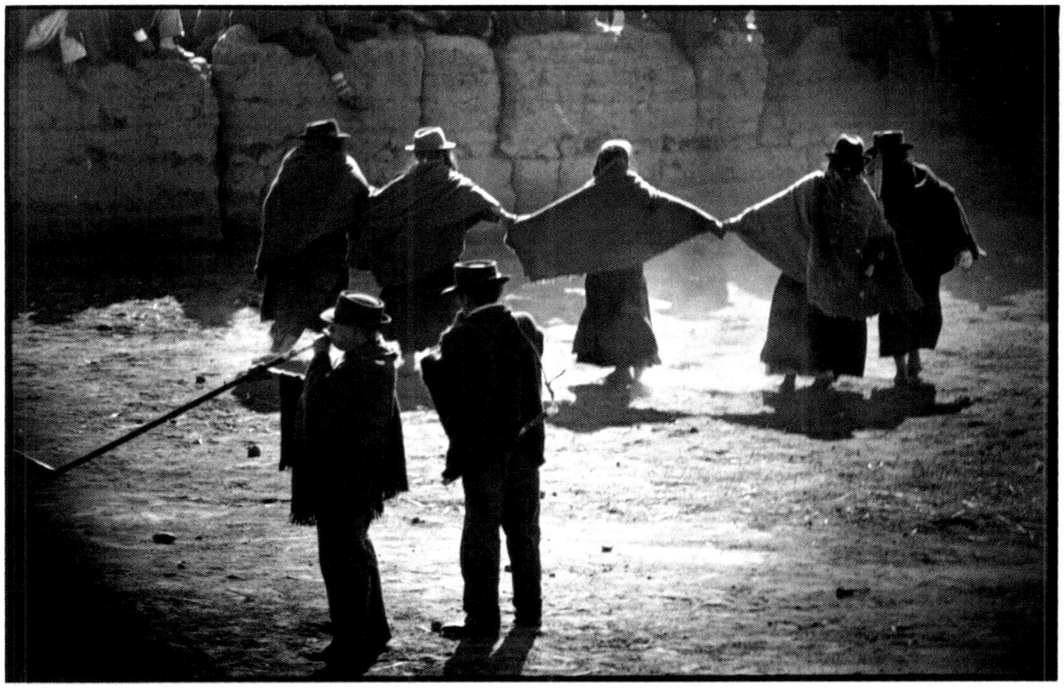

Hugo Cifuentes, *La danza de la bocina* (The horn dance), Ecuador, 1978

Chapter three is built around images from two books: *Fotomontador* by Josep Renau and *Cuba: Dos épocas*, with accompanying texts from Joan Fontcuberta and Alma Guillermoprieto. The Catalonian designer and painter Josep Renau produced a series of photomontages in Mexico that issued a fierce criticism of capitalism. As a complement to these images, the chapter also presents photographs from two Cuban photographers from the same period: Constantino Arias and Raúl Corrales.

The fourth chapter includes the work of two great Mexican photojournalists who have been active since the 1940s: Nacho López and Héctor García. Both have contributed memorable images of Mexico City. Carlos Monsiváis, a remarkable witness to the life of this great city, wrote the highly stimulating text.

In the chapter entitled "Poetry of the Onlooker," there are images from five books and five authors: *Sueños de papel* by Graciela Iturbide, *Retornos a Oapan* by Abbas, *Sendas del Ecuador* by Hugo Cifuentes, *Al paso del tiempo* by José Luis Neyra, and *Casa Santa* by Rafael Doniz. These photographers, each with a different approach and style, express a poetry through images which essayist and poet Verónica Volkow helps us unravel in her accompanying article.

If all generalizations are not made in vain, we could say that the atmosphere and character of the peoples of Latin America have suggested a wonderful theme for our photography: people and their relationships. In the book *Historia natural de las cosas*, which features fifty photographers, objects are given a voice to speak—of those who made them, or those who own them, of the people who arranged them or simply saw them and decided to record them. Accompanying these images is the text written for the original edition by poet and novelist Álvaro Mutis.

The last chapter is based on the book *Dulce sudor amargo* by Brazilian photographer Miguel Rio Branco. He uses color to speak with eloquence and depth of the horror, the pain, and the beauty that shape the backdrop for his pictures of the northeastern Brazilian city of Salvador. Roberto Tejada, editor, poet, and essayist, examines these images and offers his interpretation.

*Mucho sol* is the title Manuel Álvarez Bravo gave to his book published in Río de Luz. We are not including it here since *Aperture* recently dedicated an entire issue to don Manuel. He has taught us all a great deal: to look with our eyes wide open and also to look with our eyes closed. Above all, he has enlightened us with *mucho sol*.

—Pablo Ortiz Monasterio

Translated from the Spanish by Jana Schroeder

# Río de Luz

## THE ORIGINS OF RÍO DE LUZ

### By Víctor Flores Olea

Prominent in the cultural backdrop to the appearance of Río de Luz is Mexico's grand visual-arts tradition, primarily its mural paintings and its engraving; deep-rooted traditions that have produced works of international impact. The success of these established artistic expressions raised the question of promoting the modern medium of photography. The presence in Mexico of important photographers such as Manuel Álvarez Bravo and younger artists such as Graciela Iturbide, and their antecedents Edward Weston and Tina Modotti of the 1920s, made the idea of showcasing the work of contemporary Mexican photographers, photographers certain to have something to say and to produce work of unquestionable quality and visual strength, seem more than natural. In the early 1980s, too, interest in photography exploded in Mexico (as it did in other countries during the same period). The medium won considerable popularity, and passion for this "new" form of expression spread.

In this context, a desire was born for a systematic presentation of the work of several generations of Mexican photographers, both recognized artists and young talents, to advance this art toward the recognition that had been reached by other modes of visual expression. After several casual meetings, Pedro Meyer, Pablo Ortiz Monasterio, and the present author decided to propose a series of photographic publications to the important Mexican publisher, El Fondo de Cultura Económica. These books would offer impeccable quality at an affordable price that would allow them to be widely distributed. The intention was not to create art objects but to present art through the book format. Jaime García Terres, then the director of El Fondo de Cultura Económica, accepted our proposal with generosity and enthusiasm. He even offered the series its title: Río de Luz.

As we prepared the project it soon became clear that the collection could not be limited to the work of Mexican photographers but should become a vehicle and point of departure, if possible, for representative Latin American photography. Cultural links and ties between photographers in different countries, who had often collaborated in previous exhibitions and joint projects, made Río de Luz the symbol and in some way the emblem of photography across the continent, also experiencing an extraordinary boom.

What were the general characteristics of the publications we planned? We did not try to speak for a single photographic school or tendency, but it suddenly became clear that what was most interesting and important in Latin American photography was work that expressed the continent's historical "moment," its historical frustrations (the era of the dictatorships throughout the 1970s), and its social conflicts, as well as the strength of its peoples, the originality of their ceremonies, their beauty, and the beauty of the natural environment. It was not a question of trying to "formalize" beautiful objects around us, but of expressing the dramatic force of the social conflicts that define us. Work that did so sometimes fell into pessimism, sometimes renewed our vigor for the fight. And Río de Luz became a collection that spanned a wide, multigenerational time frame and a broad geographic space. It became clear that the photography of these regions has its own particular language, defined aesthetic, and unique perspective on the world—on history, on social conflict, and on their images. It demonstrates a clear solidarity with and understanding of the unfortunate, an ability to protest injustice and violence, and a sense of humor about the flagrant divisions between rich and poor, success and failure, the privileged and the destitute. These are among the qualities esteemed in the collection.

One of the most intense characteristics of Río de Luz was its attempt to bring aesthetics and history into harmony, to present them side by side. Supporting this effort, another form of thinking assumed a central role in the project: each publication included an essay, and these essays were created by recognized writers and scholars from Mexico, Latin America, and Spain, so that the dignity of the images was coupled with the dignity of reflection and response to them. Río de Luz: a collection of photographs informed by an impulse artistic and humane. In completing its cycle, the series paved the way for other outstanding series, projects, and initiatives. To younger generations, Río de Luz undoubtedly inspired a new calling to the art of photography.

Translated from the Spanish by Susan Briante

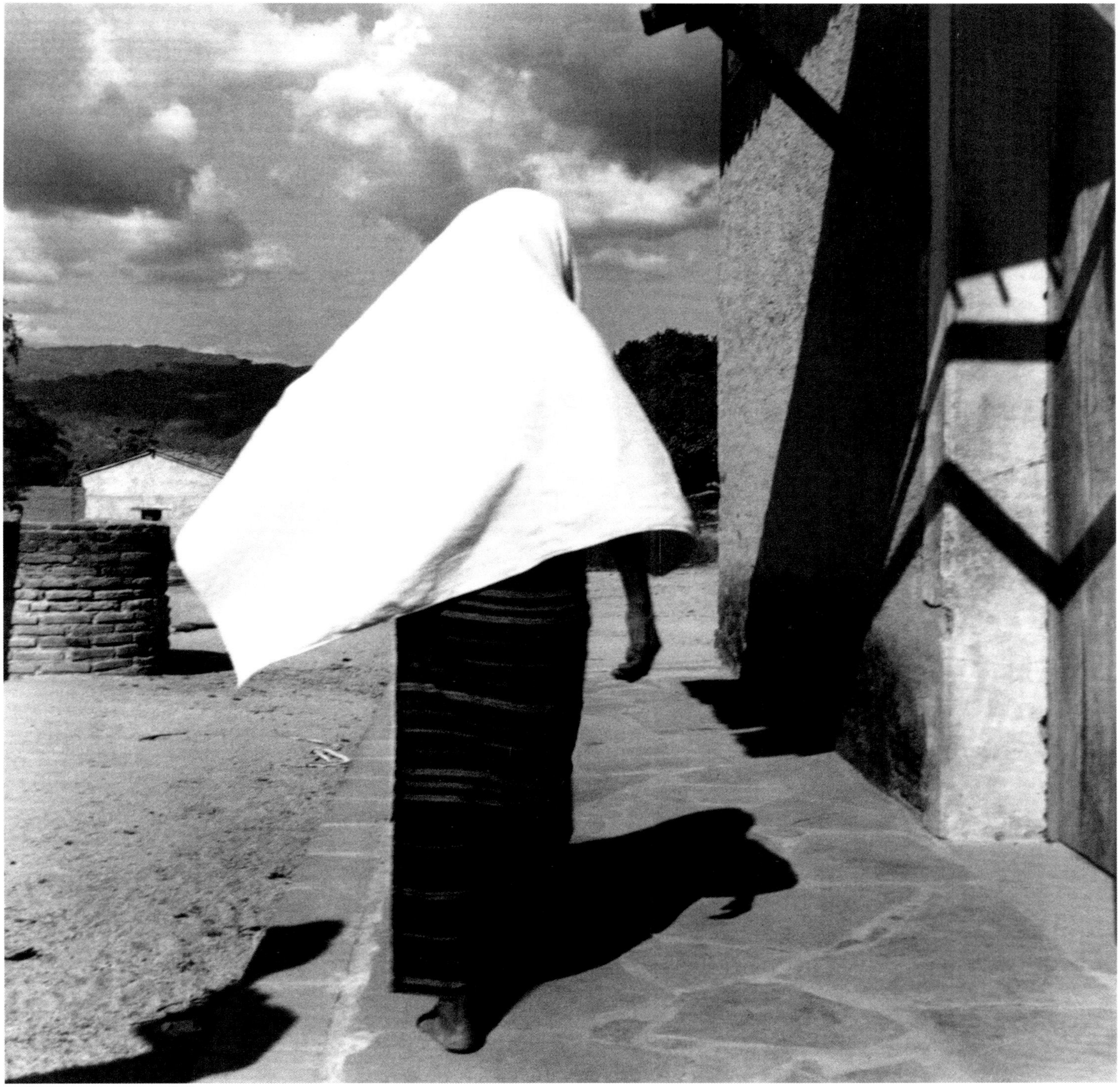

Mariana Yampolsky, *Huipil de tapar* (Covered with a *huipil*),
Pinotepa Nacional, Oaxaca, Mexico, 1954

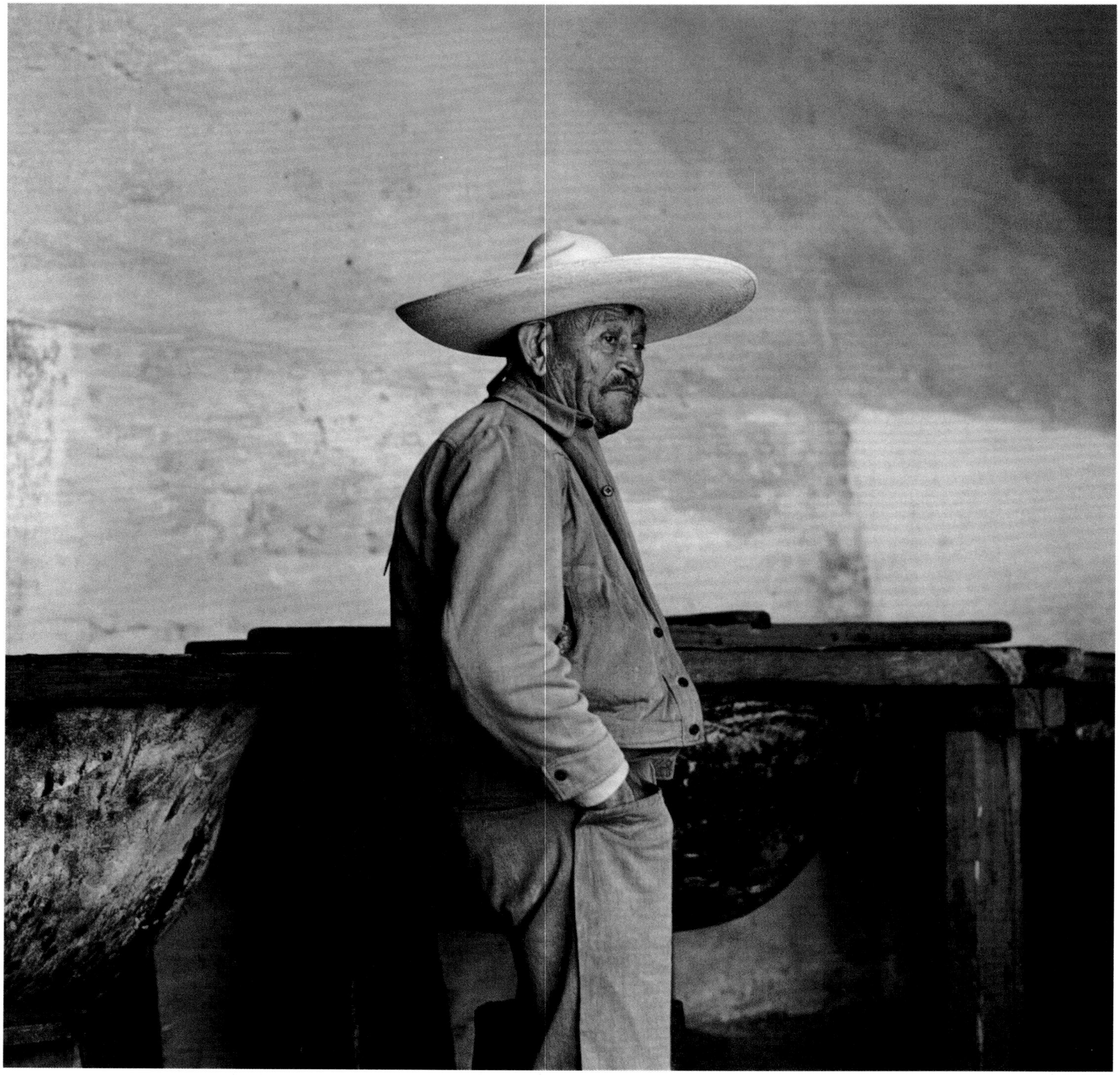

Mariana Yampolsky, *Mayordomo* (Majordomo), Hacienda La Noria, Tlaxcala, Mexico, 1978

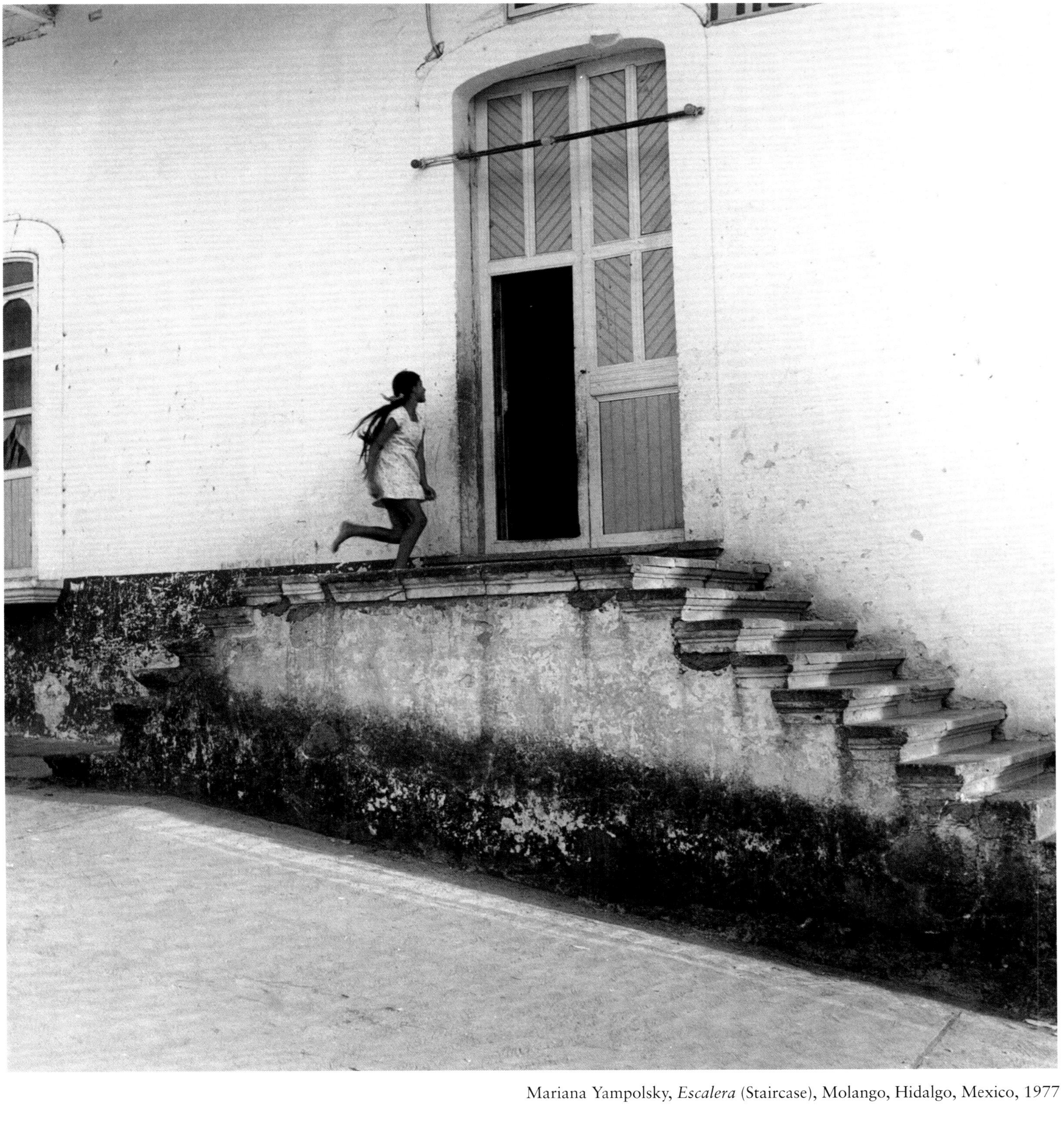

Mariana Yampolsky, *Escalera* (Staircase), Molango, Hidalgo, Mexico, 1977

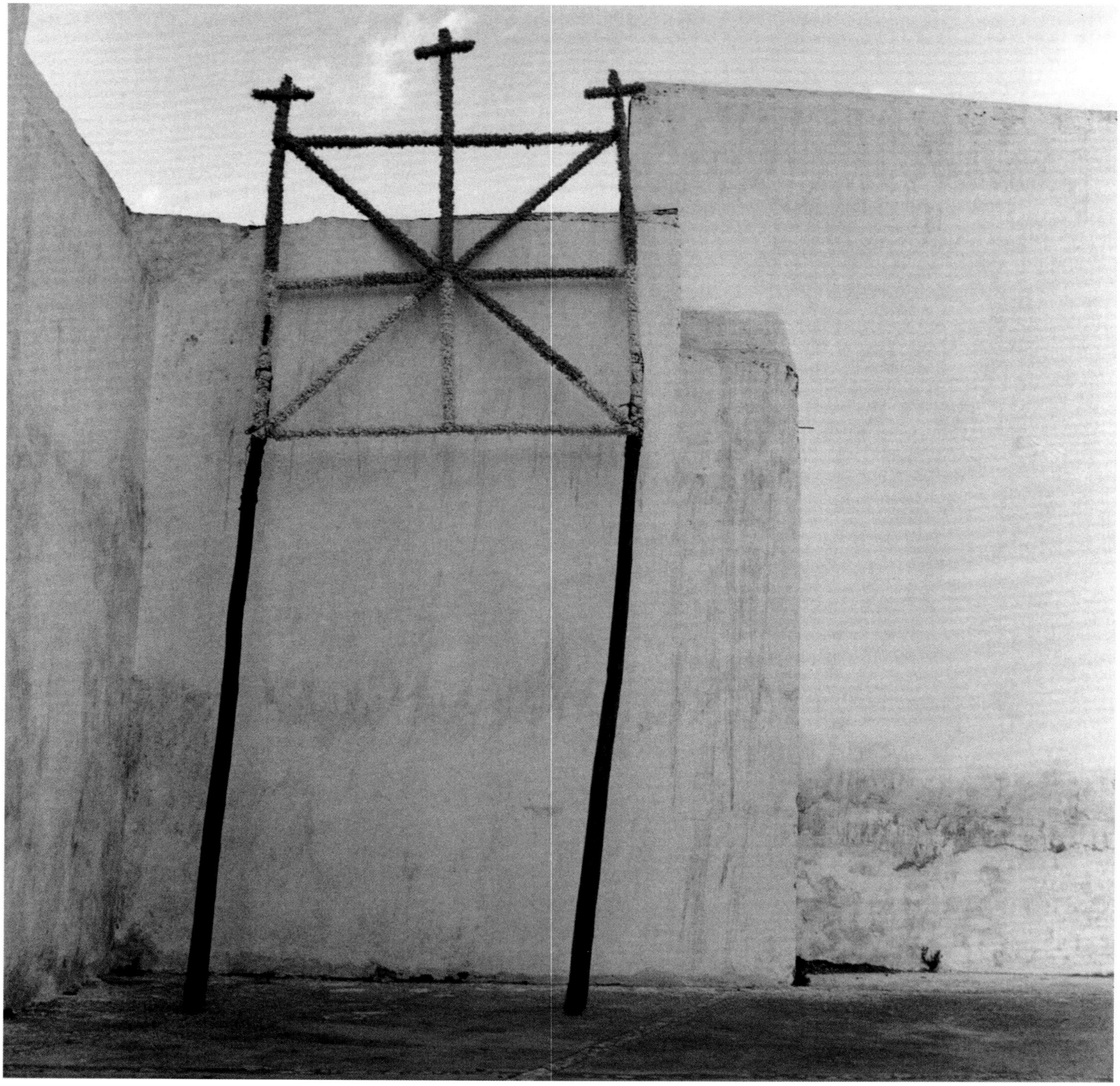

Mariana Yampolsky, *Arco ceremonial* (Ceremonial arch), Tlaxcala, Mexico, n.d.

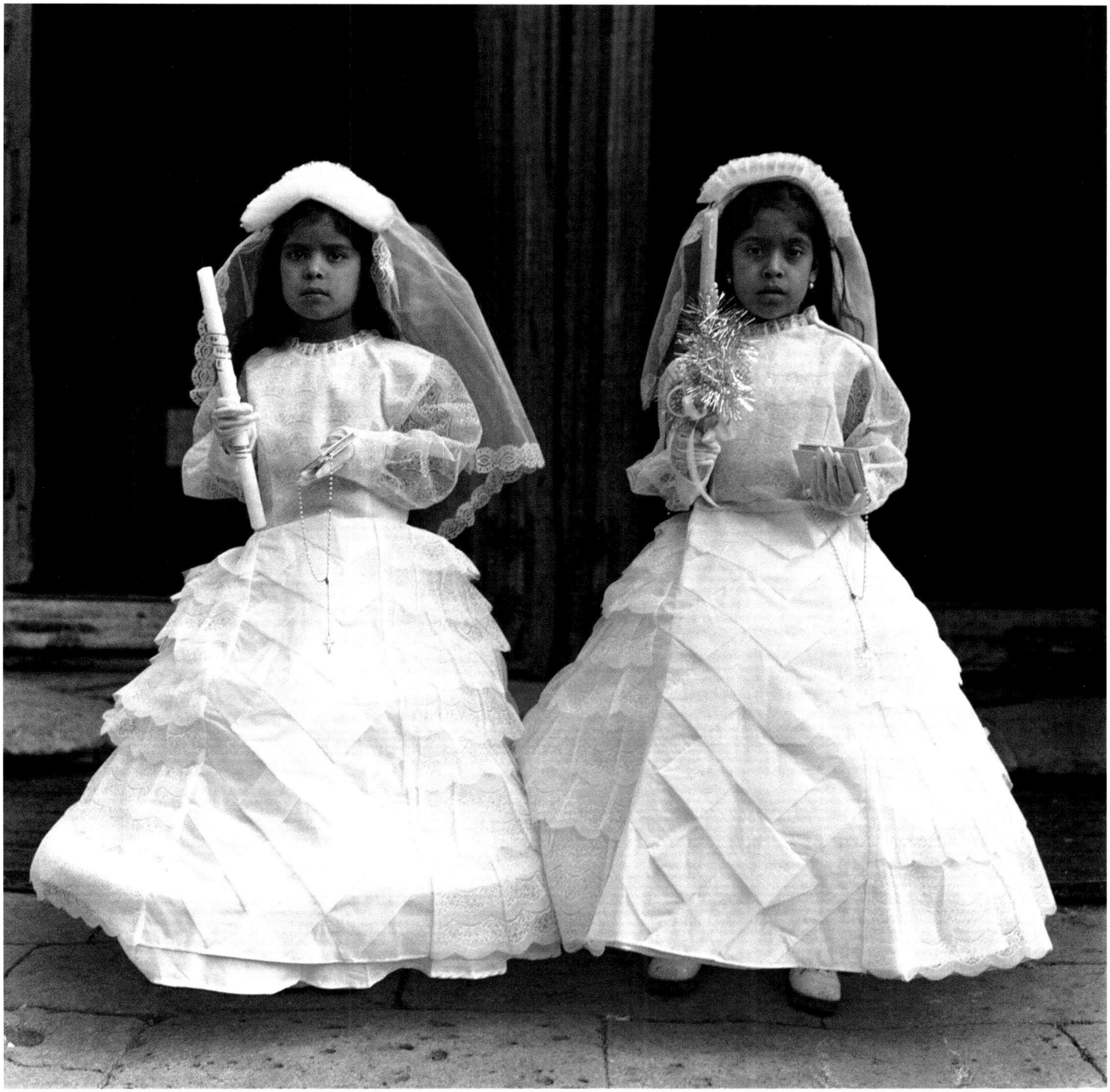

Lázaro Blanco, *La comunión primera* (First Communion), Taxco, Guerrero, Mexico, 1976

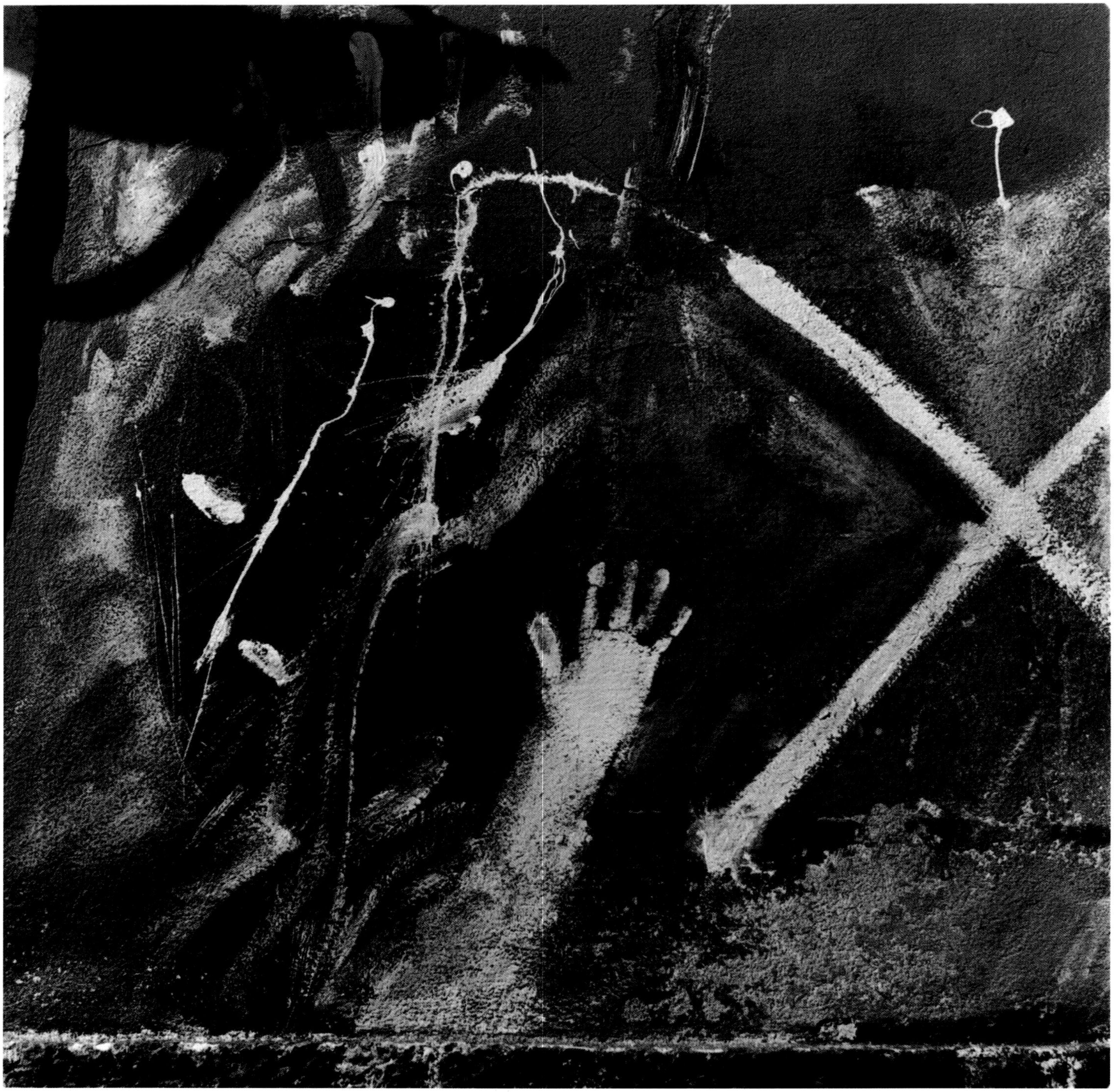

Lázaro Blanco, *La protesta* (The protest), Mexico City, Mexico, 1973

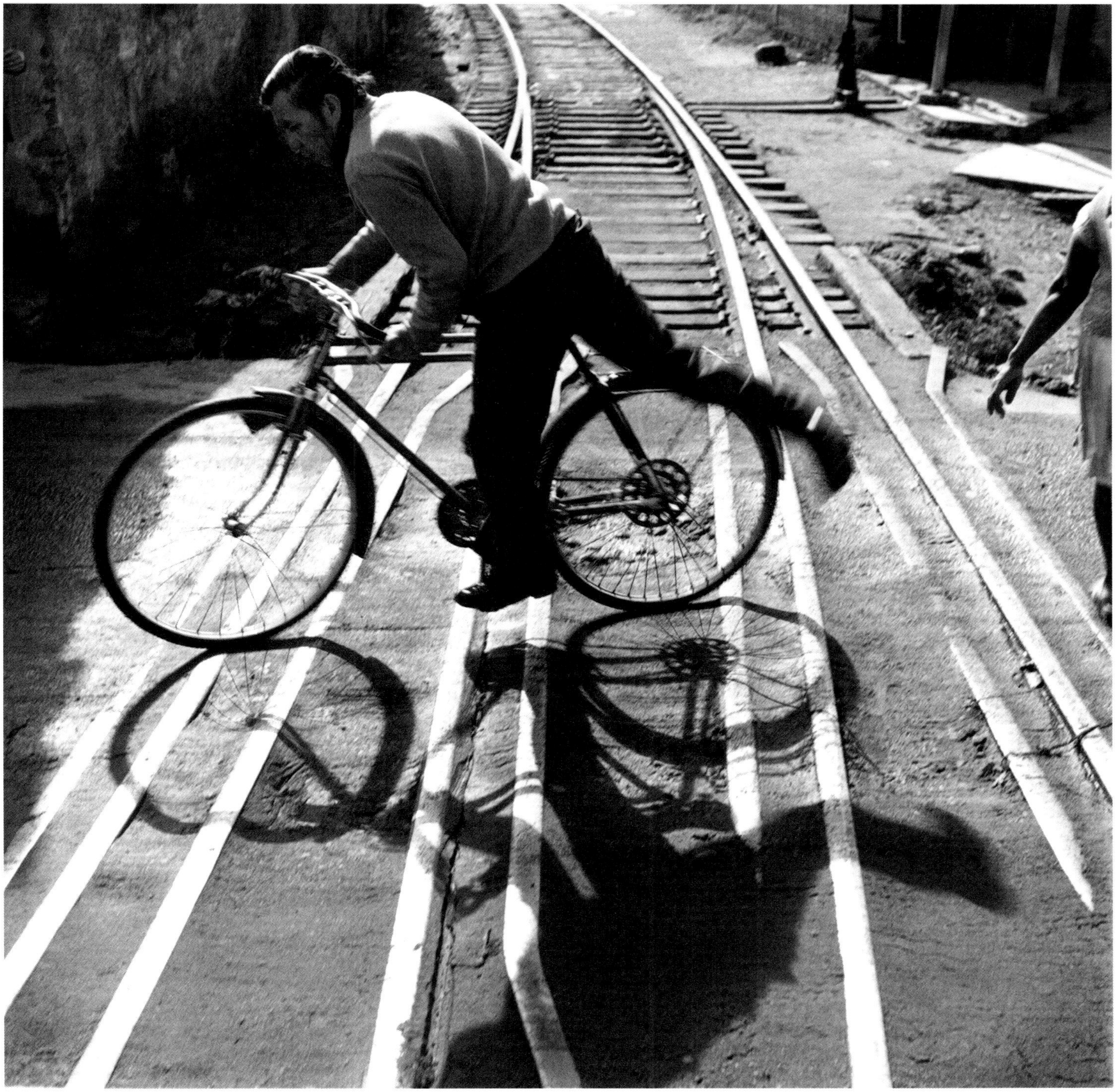

Lázaro Blanco, *Saltándose las normas* (Breaking the rules),
San Marín Texmelucán, Puebla, Mexico, 1974

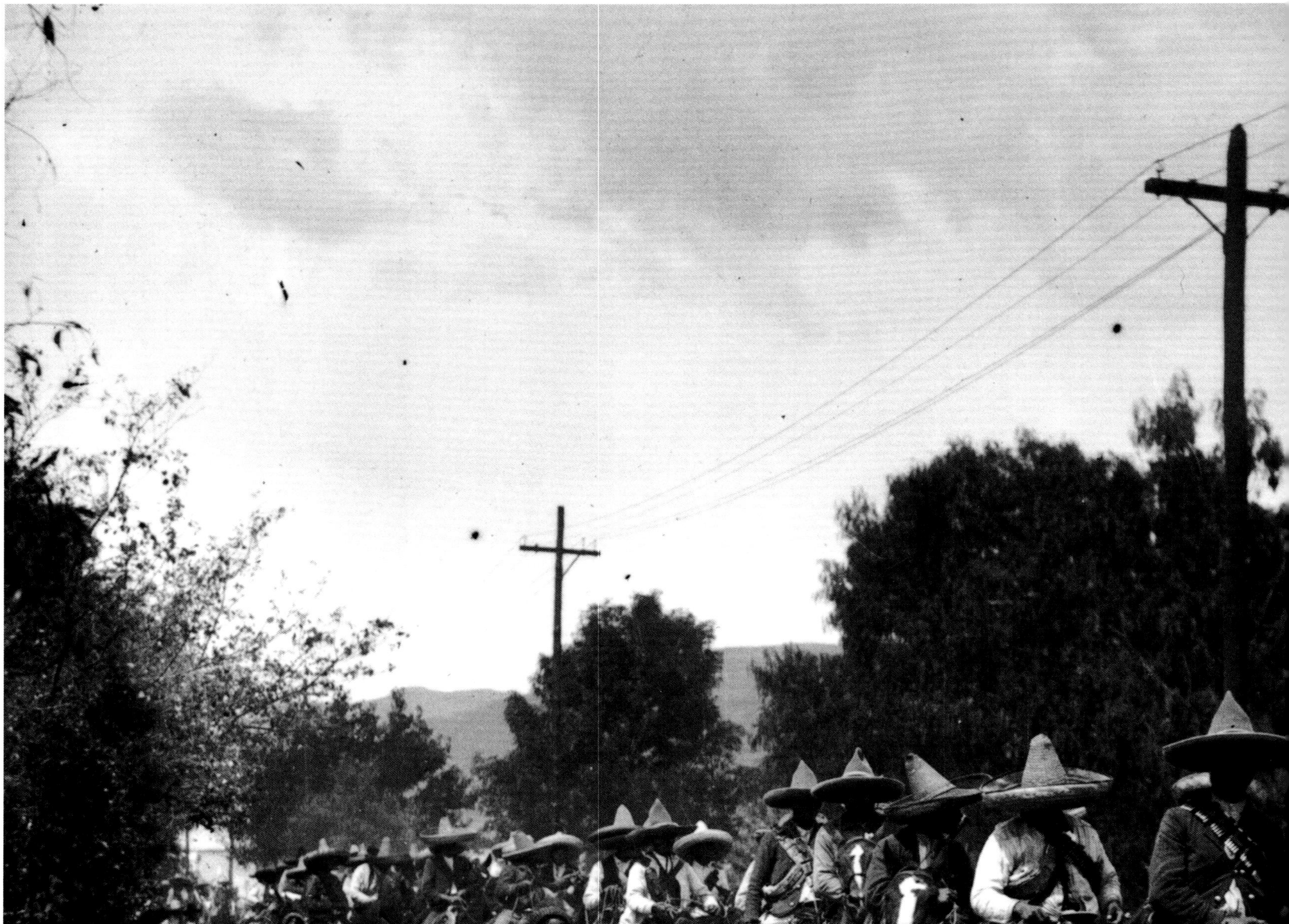

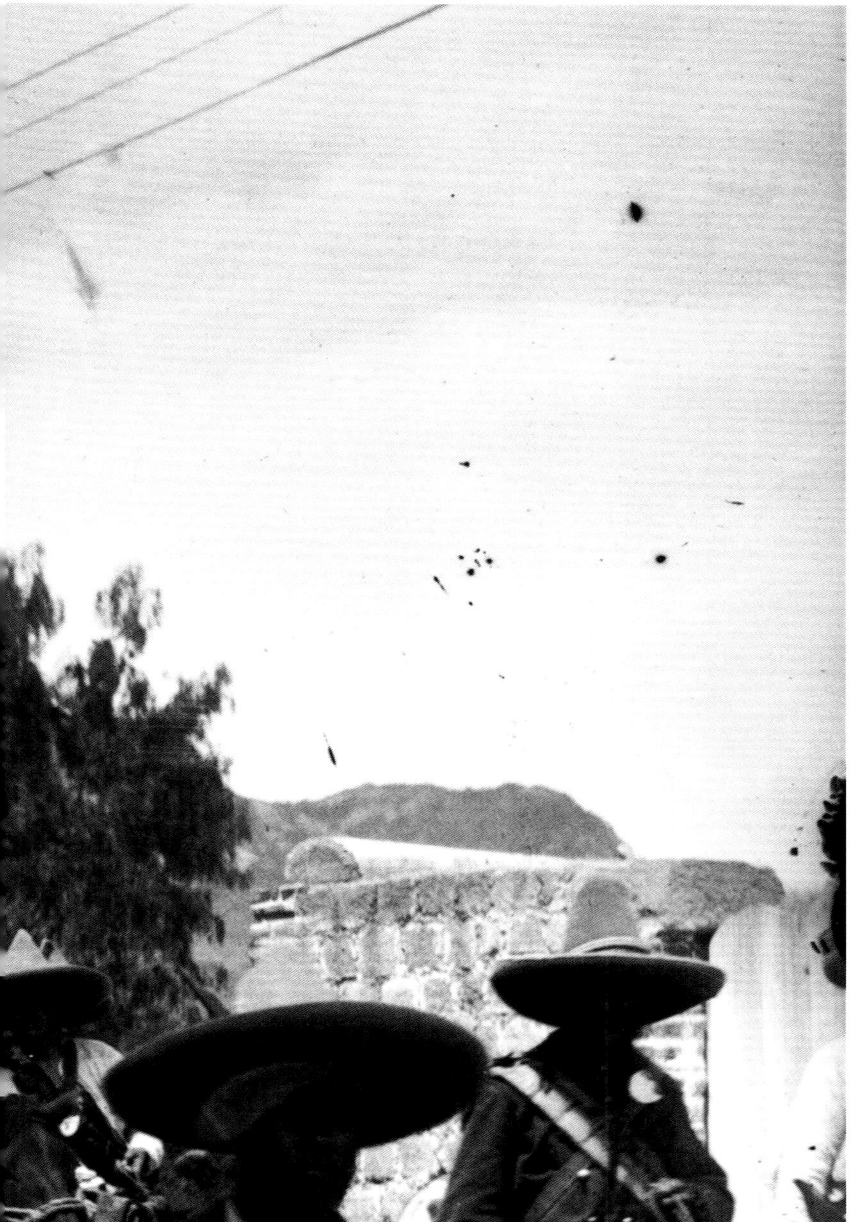

# Revolutions

## THE CASASOLA ARCHIVE, PEDRO MEYER, AND ARGENTINIAN PHOTOGRAPHERS IN THE RÍO DE LUZ COLLECTION

### By Raquel Tibol

Although they were made in different times and places, the images that constitute the following three books in the Río de Luz collection: *Jefes, héroes y caudillos* (Leaders, heroes, and caudillos), *Espejo de espinas* (Mirror of thorns), and *Democracia vigilada* (Keeping an eye on democracy), share the quality of having established certain truths for the public to know and interpret. They were dedicated respectively to a section of the immense Casasola Archive, to the author-photographer Pedro Meyer, and to aspects of the tragedy of the Argentinian people under military dictatorship, as documented by thirty photojournalists. In the photographers' close encounter with social struggle, they tacitly counted on the broad democratization of public sensibilities that had been encouraged first by illustrated magazines and newspapers, and later by television news programs. But one should note a difference: where the Casasola Archive and the Argentinian political conflict were witnessed and documented by photojournalists, *Espejo de espinas* examined the notions of style and aesthetic autonomy, principles that photographers who felt the need to inform and illustrate, to warn or denounce, had never earlier considered as a mode by which to do so.

The work of Agustín Víctor Casasola, as both a photographer and the organizer of a vast photo archive, has been well known in the United States and other countries for over a decade. From 1984 through 1987, *El Mundo de Agustín Casasola* (The world of Agustín Casasola), a medium-sized exhibition, toured various U.S. cities—Washington, New York, San Antonio, Los Angeles, Chicago, Tucson, Santa Fe, and Houston—then continued on through Canada (Montreal, Calgary, and Vancouver) and finally to London. Like the book that concerns us, the exhibition presented scenes of armed struggle against factions that had succeeded in gaining power for brief and always violent periods.

Casasola was born on July 28, 1874, in Mexico City. When he was six years old his father died, and at a very young age Casasola went to work in typography and bindery workshops. By the end of the nineteenth century he had become a reporter for the most important newspapers in the city. Casasola soon decided to exchange words for pictures. Photographers were then low on the

*(continued on page 16)*

Agustín Víctor Casasola, "*Adelita*," Federal troops leave to fight the rebels in the north, Mexico, July 1913

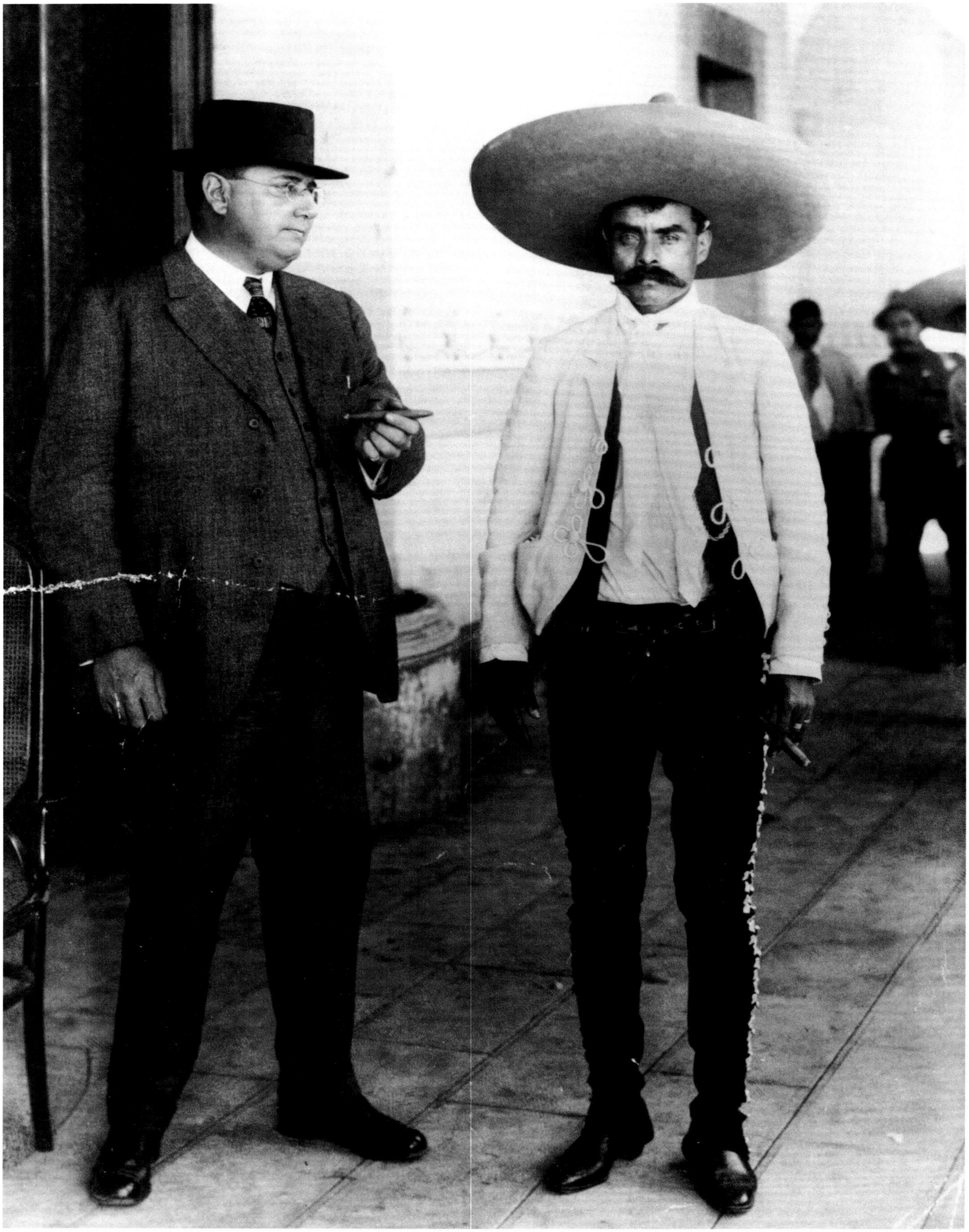

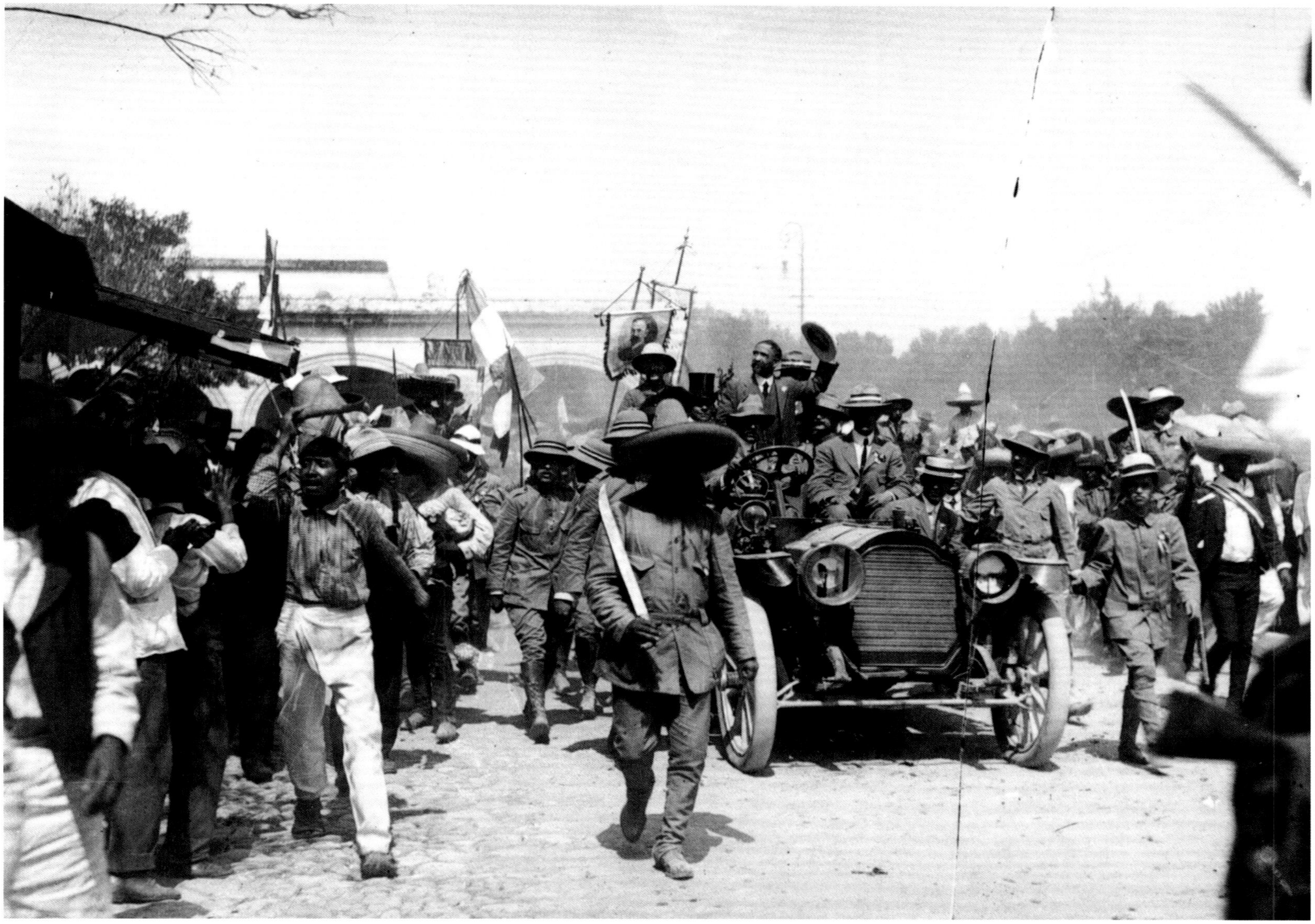

Agustín Víctor Casasola, Francisco I. Madero on his arrival to the city of Cuernavaca, escorted by the chiefs of the South Army (Zapata at the far right), Morelos, Mexico, June 1911

*Opposite*: Agustín Víctor Casasola, Mr. George C. Carothers, American consul, and Emiliano Zapata, awaiting the arrival of Francisco Villa, Xochimilco, Mexico, December 1914

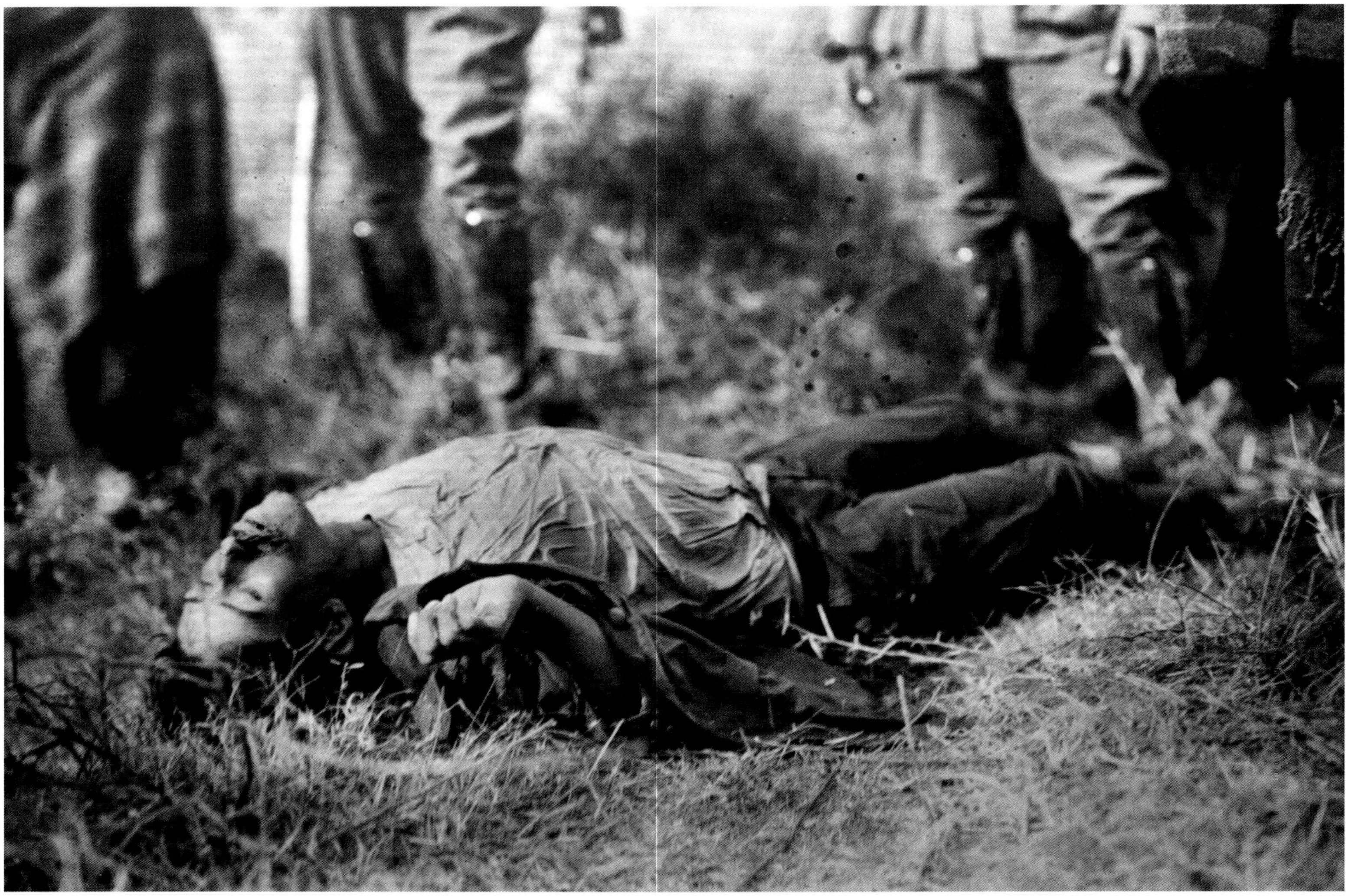

Agustín Víctor Casasola, Revolution chief killed in the battles of Palo Verde, Jalisco, Mexico, 1924

journalism totem pole, and most worked anonymously; this allowed him to acquire and use the work of his colleagues (including the negatives) without crediting them individually. There was no abuse or ill intention on his part; news photographers had not begun to defend their rights as authors, and it was rare to find one who systematically organized his materials. Meanwhile there was a constant demand for photographs covering the most diverse fields.

In 1912, then, Casasola founded the Agencia Fotográfica Mexicana (Mexican photographic agency). The agency collected his own work, the work of his brother Miguel, as well as that of Hugo Breme, Eduardo Melhado, Manuel Ramos, Víctor León, Luis Santamaría, Gerónimo Hernández, Samuel Tinoco, José María, and Abraham Lupercio. Such outstanding figures as Charles E. Waite were also represented. Following Casasola's death in 1938, his sons and grandsons added to the holdings, so that by 1976, when their files were acquired by the Instituto Nacional de Antropología e Historia, the number of images was enormous: more than 1,000,000.

To select the eighty-four reproductions that appear in *Jefes, héroes y caudillos*, and to arouse new interest in Mexico's best-known collection of documentary photographs, Flora Lara Klahr and Marco A. Hernández reviewed some 700 Casasola Archive negatives documenting the period from the fall of the dictatorship of Porfirio Díaz (1910) to the end of the government of Álvaro Obregón (1924). Flora Lara Klahr wrote in her essay in the book that their intention was to "express all the pathos, the dignity or the uncertainty of a people at war," without resorting to photographs that had been widely reproduced, not only in print but

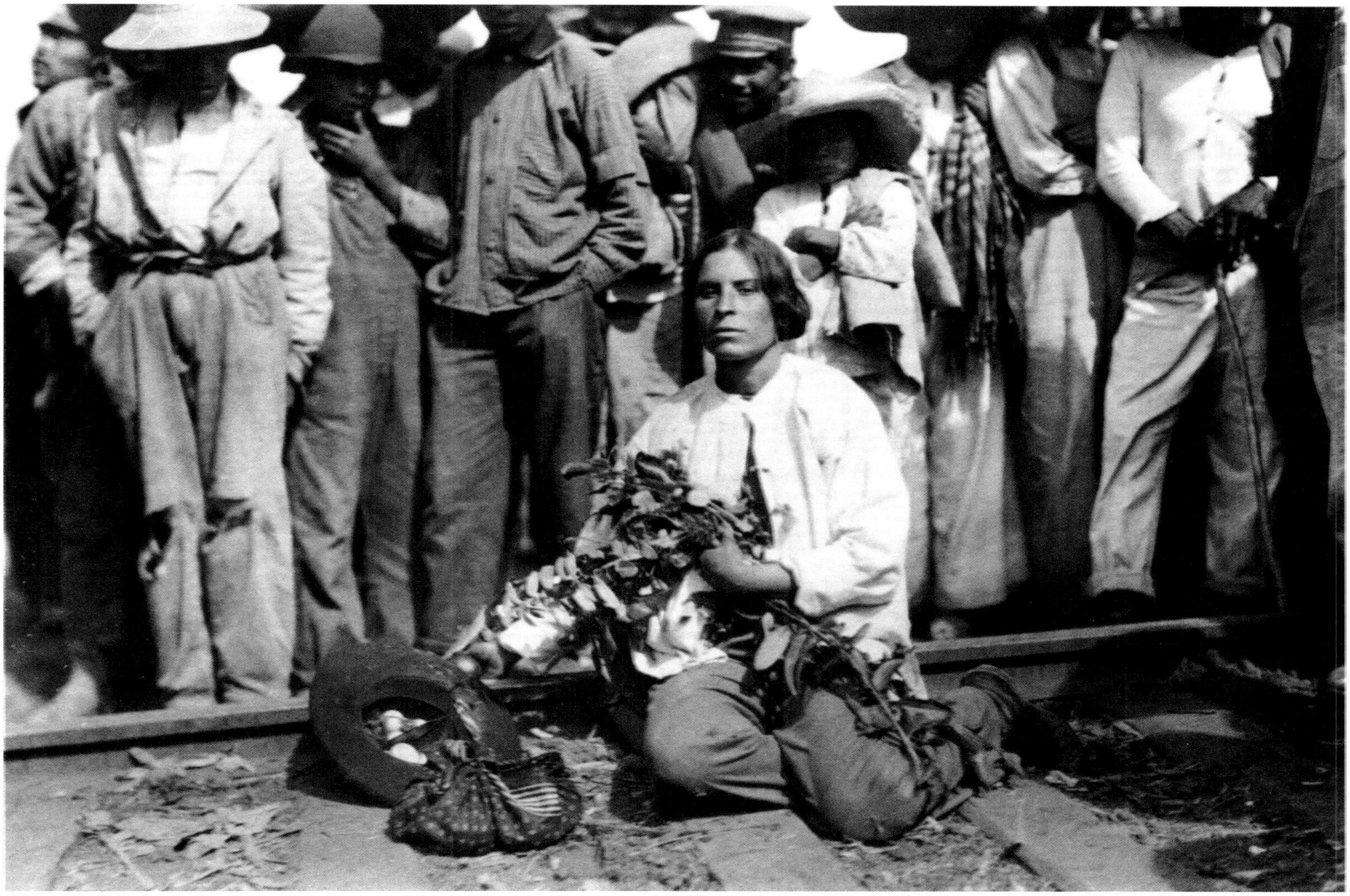

Agustín Víctor Casasola, Maria Zavala, "La destroyer," helped the soldiers to die a good death, Mexico, 1927

by painters and graphic and sketch artists who had used these images as models. Tilted toward the past—it could not be otherwise—the selection successfully rekindled the visual tensions of the moment, helping viewers to understand that these photographic testimonies were captured from inside the events they documented. From caudillos to troops, there is a change not only in the personalities photographed but in the sympathies of those behind the camera.

The best contemporary Mexican photographers acknowledge Edward Weston, Tina Modotti, and Paul Strand as their visual antecedents, and Pedro Meyer certainly studied these artists' work, as well as its Mexican derivations, principally the work of Manuel Álvarez Bravo. He was able to situate himself both historically and aesthetically as a result. The photographs in *Espejo de espinas* are of two kinds: those that found visual value in situations set in motion by others, and those in which the photographer arranged objects and people in symbolic or transformational scenes. The photographs were not arranged chronologically, but synthesized twenty years of work, from 1965 to 1985, a time when Meyer used no camera tricks or laboratory tricks; his commitment was concentrated on refining the visible.

Meyer was never a press photographer, but in 1978 he got himself accredited to a newspaper so that he could immerse himself in the revolution in Nicaragua, documenting both guerrilla activity and government repression before the rebel victory in 1979. Meyer's photographs of the anti-Somoza guerrillas, he said, with their guns and their love of country, "are not those of a tourist who visits with the guerrillas; [my pictures] try to do away with

*(continued on page 21)*

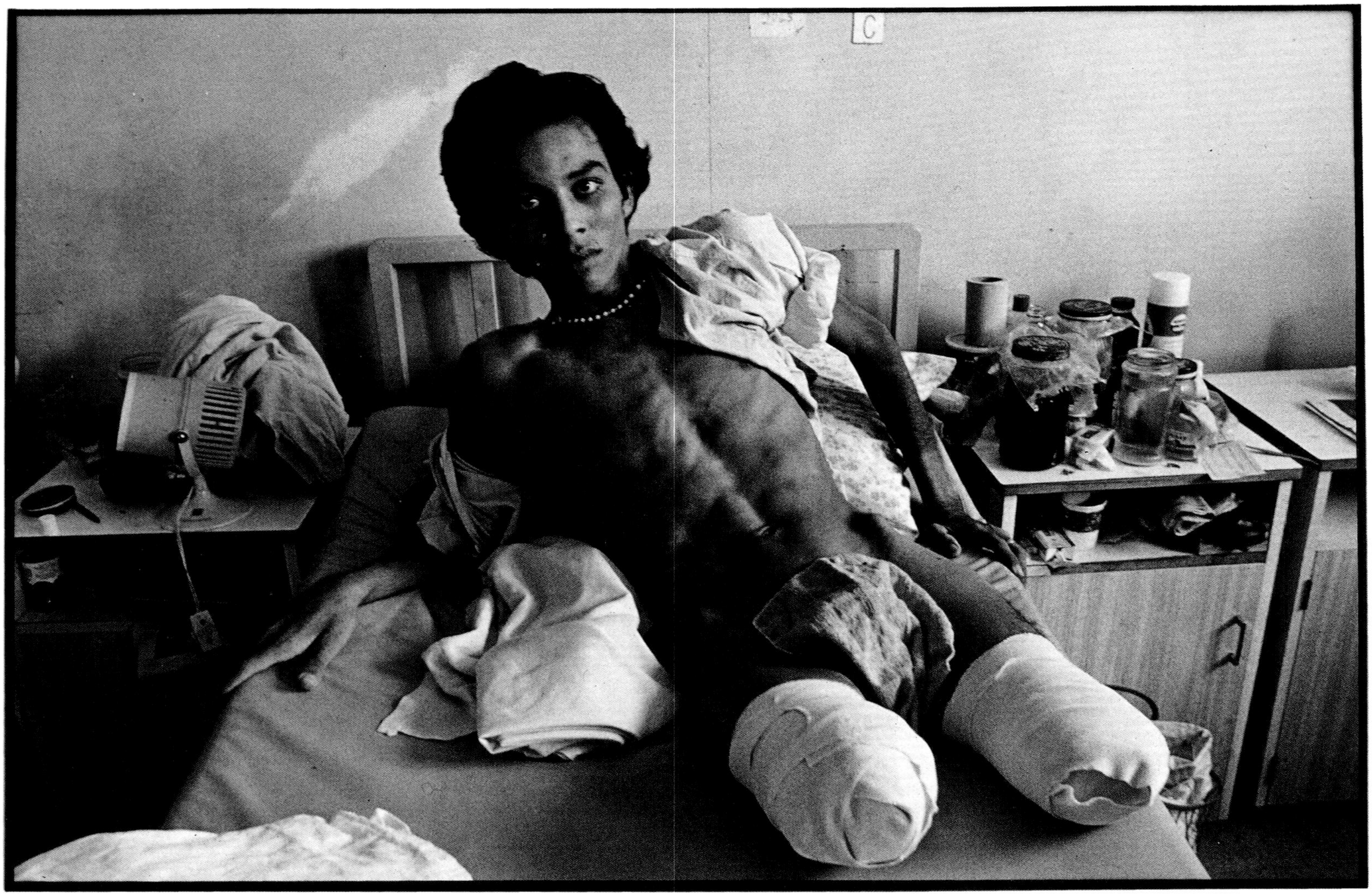


Pedro Meyer, *El guerrillero herido* (Wounded guerilla fighter), Nicaragua, 1979

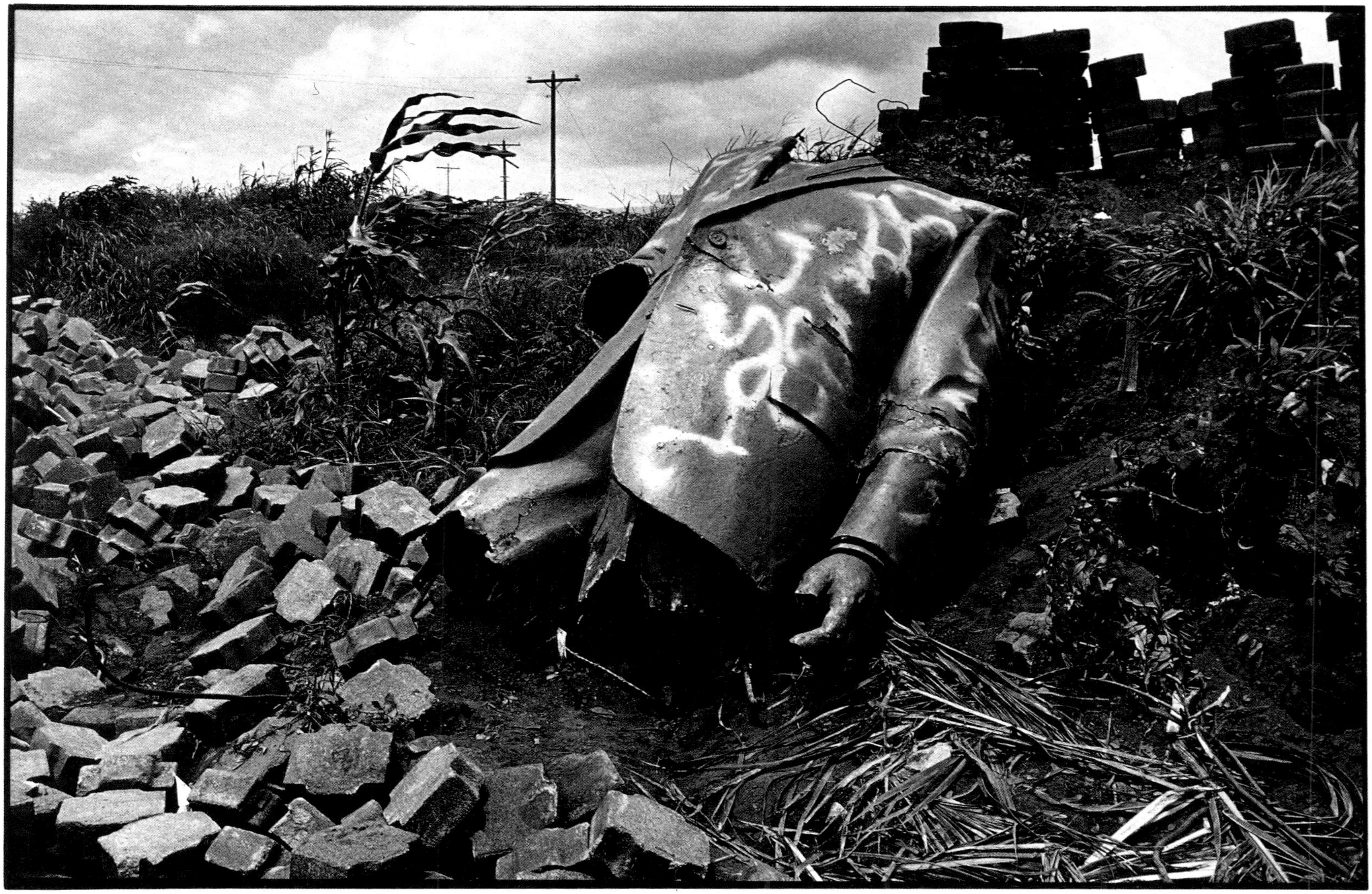

Pedro Meyer, *Somoza destruido* (Somoza destroyed), Nicaragua, 1979

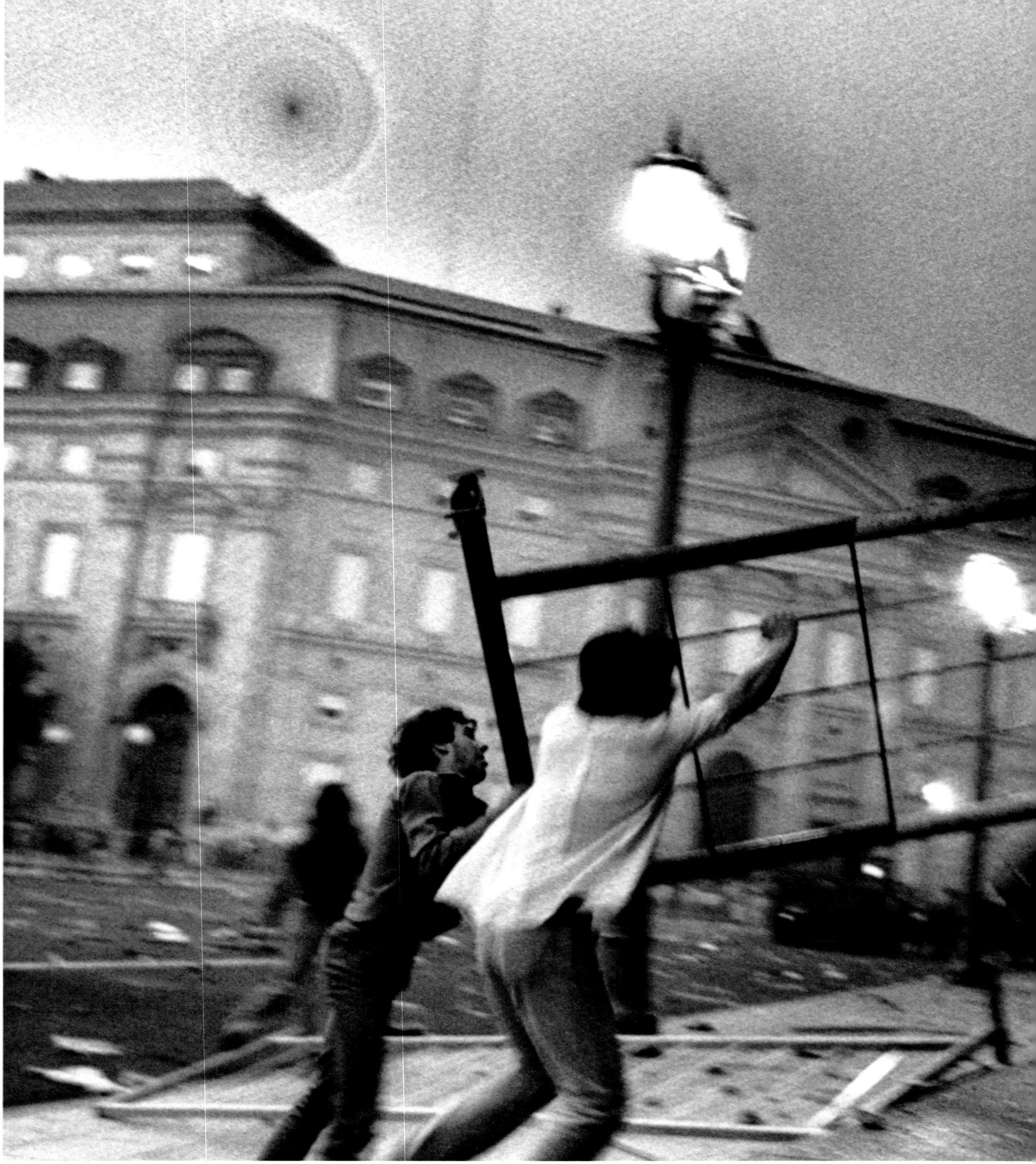

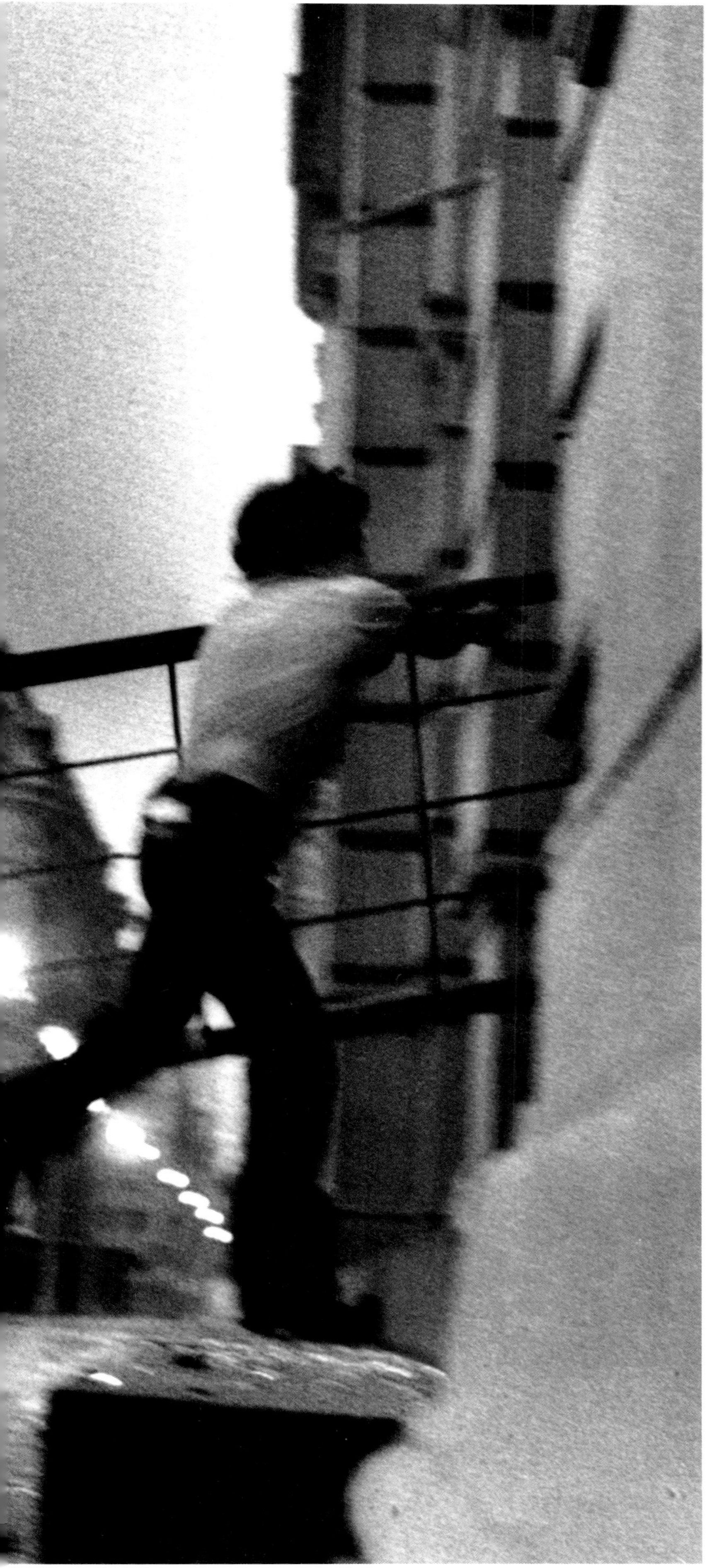

the stereotyped idea transmitted by the media of the malicious guerrilla fighter, maladapted and resentful; I place him as a person with valid ideals and a commitment to the struggle. I tried to capture the contradiction that Nicaragua experienced. Photography is a form of participation. The photographer is always immersed in a concrete reality." Capturing a precise historical time and its later social consequences, the diptych of a Nicaraguan guerrilla fighter who lost both legs in one of the last battles against the corrupt regime and the fallen broken statue of Anastasio Somoza has been recognized around the world as a harsh allegory of the changes that have taken place in Latin America and elsewhere. That recognition was possible because Meyer went to his rendezvous with Central America equipped with a high degree of professionalism, and was capable of rendering undogmatic results filled with critical realism.

Works by about thirty Argentinian photographers were chosen for *Democracia vigilada*: Martín Acosta, Jorge Aguirre, Eduardo Barro, A. Becquer Casaballe, Eduardo Bottaro, Rafael Calviño, Ricardo Cárcova, Ricardo Ceppi, Rodolfo del Percio, Víctor Dimola, Eduardo Frías, Daniel García, Pablo Grinberg, Pablo Lasansky, Adriana Lestido, Guillermo Loiácono, Eduardo Longoni, Daniel Merle, Daniel Muzio, Roberto Pera, Marcelo Ranea, Jorge Manuel Rilo, Daniel Rodríguez, Enrique Rosito, Marcelo Setton, Omar Torres, Rafael Wollmann, Dani Yako, and Silvio Zuccheri. Perhaps the volume should have been titled "Illustrations for the Statistics of Terror," for over a decade after the end of what is known as the Dirty War, estimates made by the progressive sector of the Argentinian people still cause shudders: thirty thousand disappeared; ten thousand dead; ten thousand prisoners (this number is accepted as accurate by members of the military junta themselves); hundreds of thousands in exile. When nationalist euphoria broke open like a one-day flower over the war in the Malvinas (the Falkland Islands) in April 1982, the heroic Mothers of the Plaza de Mayo, who continue to this day to demand knowledge of their disappeared children and grandchildren, said, with the lucidity granted by offended and violated family love: "The Malvinas are Argentinian; they disappeared also." Two thousand young men dead in that absurd war add to the statistics given above.

Those past events continue to produce dissension in the Argentinian people, whose continuing distress prevents one from trying too hard to analyze the aesthetic of testimony in these photographs. Together they have a thorny texture that asks to be interpreted in all its nuances, without evading the sad diagnosis of events suffered by various generations of our contemporaries. Who would try to analyze these photographs formally—the composition, the planes, the converging and diverging diagonals? In each case one can only feel stunned in the face of the courage of those who, not being neutral, put themselves in the middle of the turmoil in order to exercise their right of solidarity.

Translated from the Spanish by Cola Franzen

Jorge Manuel Rilo, *Asalto al poder* (Assault on those in power), Buenos Aires, Argentina, December 1982

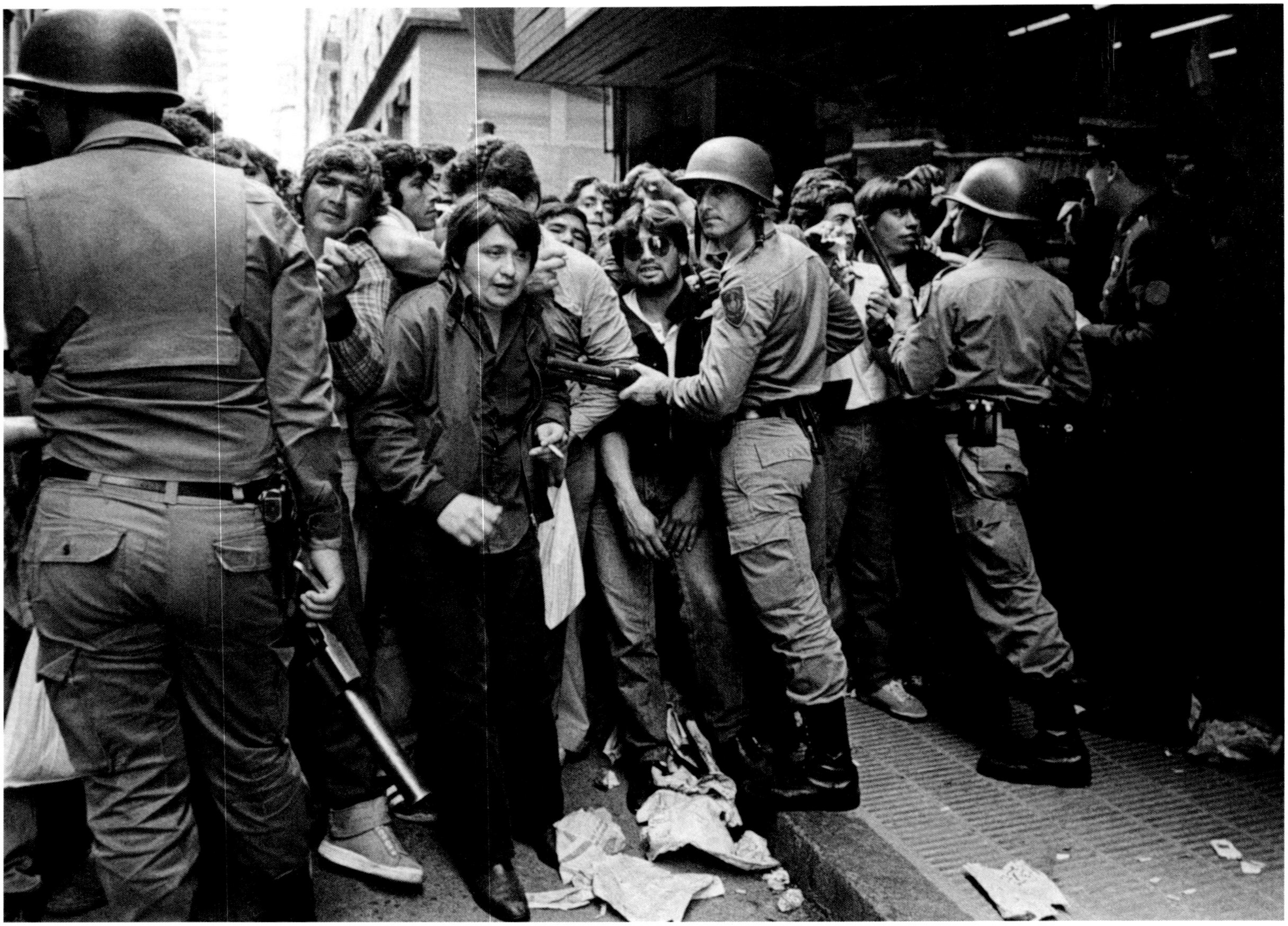

Rodolfo del Percio, Citizens waiting for their documents to be able to vote, Argentina, October 1983

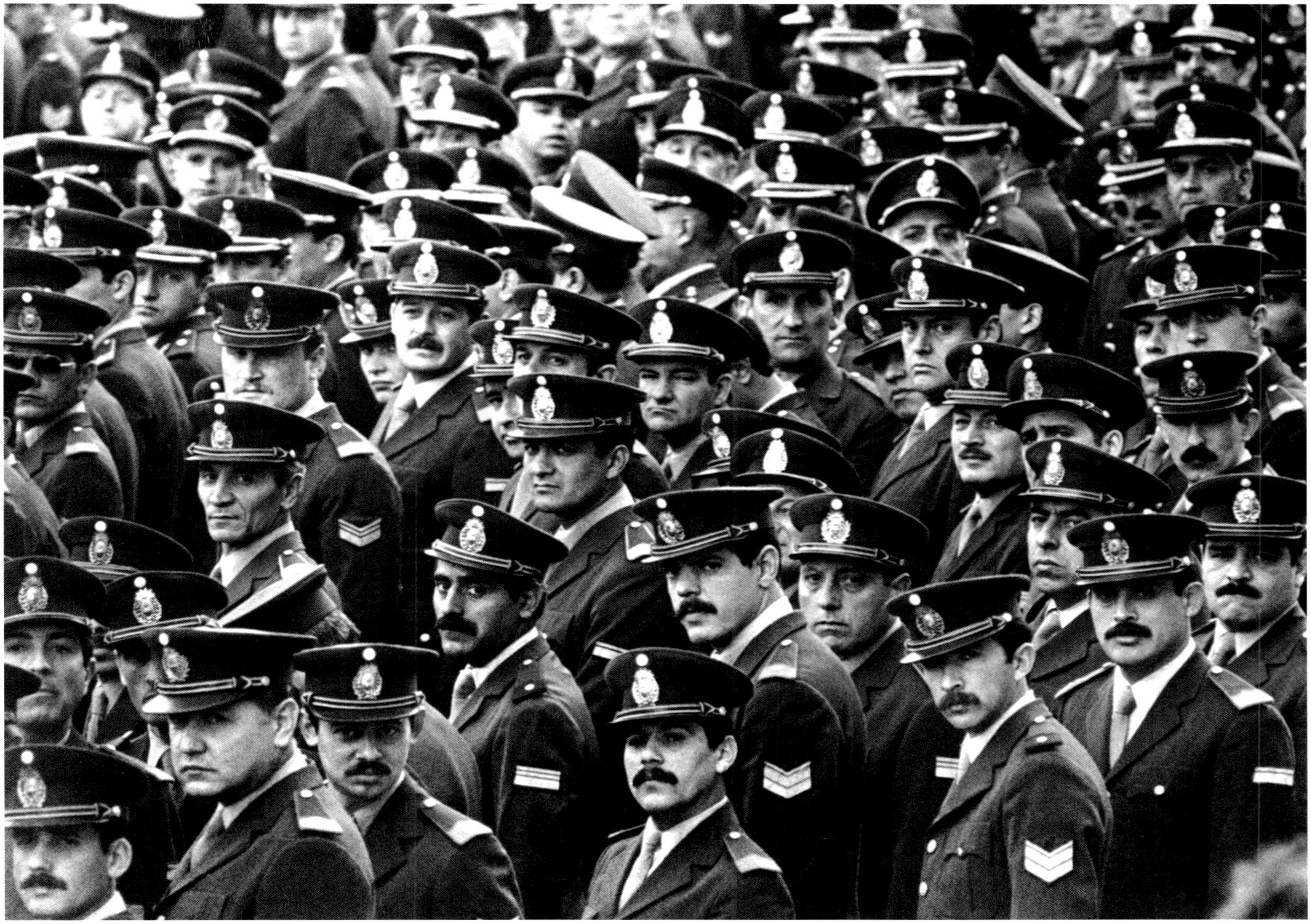

Eduardo Longoni, *El partido militar* (The military party), Argentina, n.d.

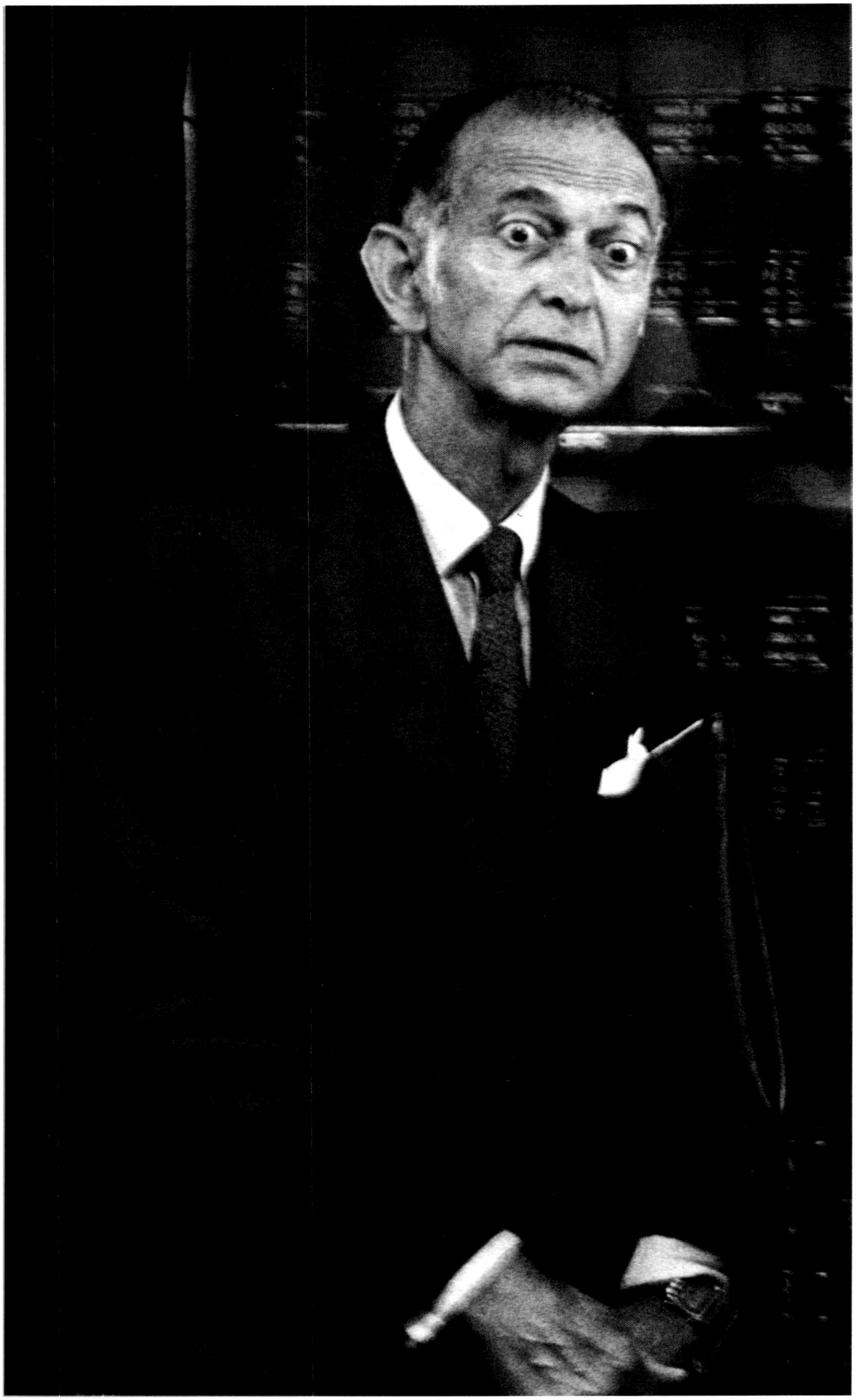

Eduardo Frías, Alfredo Martínez de Hoz, Minister
of Economics during the dictatorship, Argentina, 1984

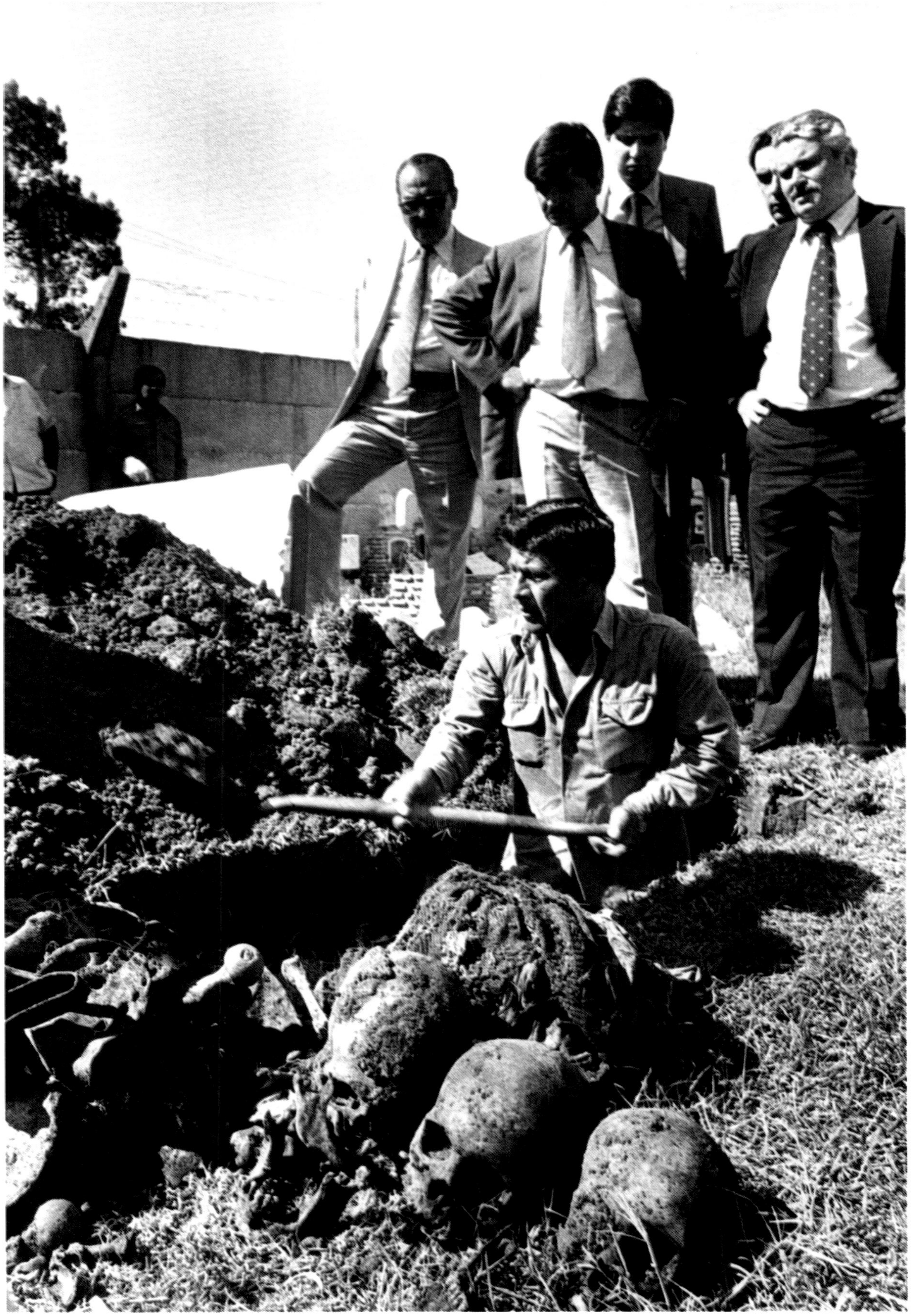

Daniel Muzio, Exhumation of anonymous bodies,
Argentina, December 1983

# The American Way of Life and Cuba

## JOSEP RENAU: "THE AMERICAN WAY OF LIFE"

### By Joan Fontcuberta

Arguably the most important artwork of this century is *Guernica*, the monumental canvas that Picasso painted for the pavilion of the Spanish Republic in the Paris Exposition of 1937. This painting might never have existed if it hadn't been commissioned by Josep Renau, then the Republic's general director of fine arts—an effective administrator and a brilliant man. Commissioning *Guernica* was one of Renau's many attempts to safeguard Spain's artistic patrimony, but his name must also go down in history because of his own activity as an artist. Always notable for its political disposition, his work can be placed between German dadaism and the Mexican muralist school, and finds its greatest expression in the cycle of photomontages entitled "The American Way of Life."

Renau, whose father was a painter and professor of drawing, became interested in photography while studying fine arts. By this time he had already become intrigued by the medium's communicative potential. A somewhat incidental experience impressed Renau deeply: in 1914, when illustrated magazines were still a luxury, he received a batch of picture publications as a gift from a captain in the merchant marine. A page from one of these drew his attention powerfully: two photographs were juxtaposed in the layout; one was an image of a palace banquet, the other a snapshot of black children in some far-off colony, their bellies swollen with hunger. On one side abundance, on the other, misery. A disturbing message emerged from the contrast. On another occasion, while Renau was clipping some photographs, two pictures of George V, King of England, by chance ended up side by side. One showed a marble bust of the monarch, the other a newspaper photograph of the king reviewing a contingent of troops preparing to embark for France. The comparison made a strong impact on Renau: here the king was a majestic Jupiter, there a small, ordinary man, bent and downcast; on the one side, propaganda, on the other, real life. The insight gained from this dialectic established the basis for Renau's later photomontages: the deconstruction of the gnoseology of the communications media of his time, and the subversion of its apparently objective content.

It was not until 1919, however, that Renau created his first photomontage, *L'Home àrtic* (Arctic man), which reflected dadaist influences and constituted a sort of symbolic self-portrait. Renau already knew John Heartfield's work by then, having come across it while glancing at the display in the window of a Valencia bookstore where there was a copy of *AIZ (Arbeiter Illustrierte Zeitung* [Workers' illustrated newspaper]) with a Heartfield photomontage on the cover. As a youth he had already experienced the effectiveness of photomontage; now the criticality inherent in the material that *AIZ* constantly published revealed its use as a political weapon. Photomontage thus became the method Renau would use for posters and book covers.

In 1938, in the middle of the Spanish Civil War, Renau did an important series of photomontages, "Los trece puntos de Negrín" (The thirteen points of Negrín). This series, commissioned by the government, illustrated thirteen points of a program to synthesize and popularize, inside and outside the country, the unifying political proposals of Prime Minister Juan Negrín's cabinet. In large format and in color, the photomontages were also meant to be shown as part of the International Art Fair in New York, scheduled for the following year, but the entrance of Francoist troops into Barcelona, where Renau had his studio, wrecked this plan. Hastily fleeing the city, the artist lost originals of "Los trece puntos de Negrín," and today only reproductions remain. Renau's photomontages differ from those of Heartfield, not only because he used color, but also because he extended their application to posters (Heartfield had concentrated on magazine covers). This meant that the graphic technique had to be showier. Formally, meanwhile, they came close to the Russian constructivist graphics of Rodchenko or Lissitsky and of the great Polish photomontagist Mieceslaw Berman. This series, in fact, anticipated the stylistic bases of "The American Way of Life."

When the Spanish Civil War ended, exile took Renau to France and then to Mexico. By the end of 1939 he had worked with David Siqueiros on the Mexico City mural for the electricians' union, *Retrato de la burguesía* (Portrait of the bourgeoisie). His rapid assimilation in his adopted country led him to become a naturalized citizen the following year. In Mexico, Renau did commercial design layouts (for an enormous collection of cinema posters, as one example) for various publishing companies, and also participated in projects of greater artistic importance to him. The proximity of the United States gave him the opportunity to observe the tremendous influence of American media propaganda firsthand, and this was the origin of "The American Way of Life."

Renau's object in this work was to clarify the contradictions of the North American capitalist system. This he would do by using the universal language of publicity—that very system's paradigm

*(continued on page 30)*

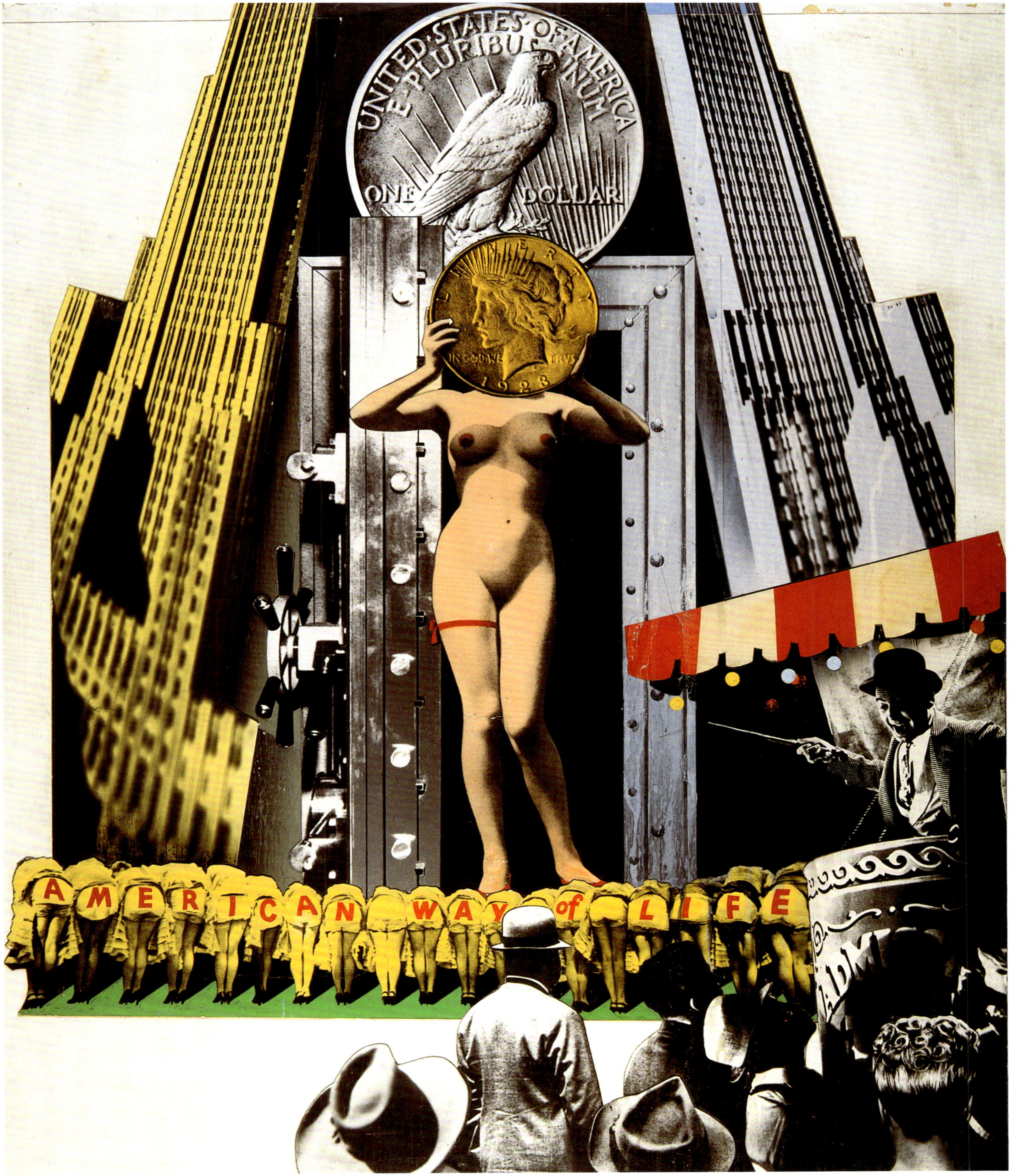


Josep Renau, *La gran desfilada* (The big parade), #2 from the series "The American Way of Life," Mexico, 1957–65

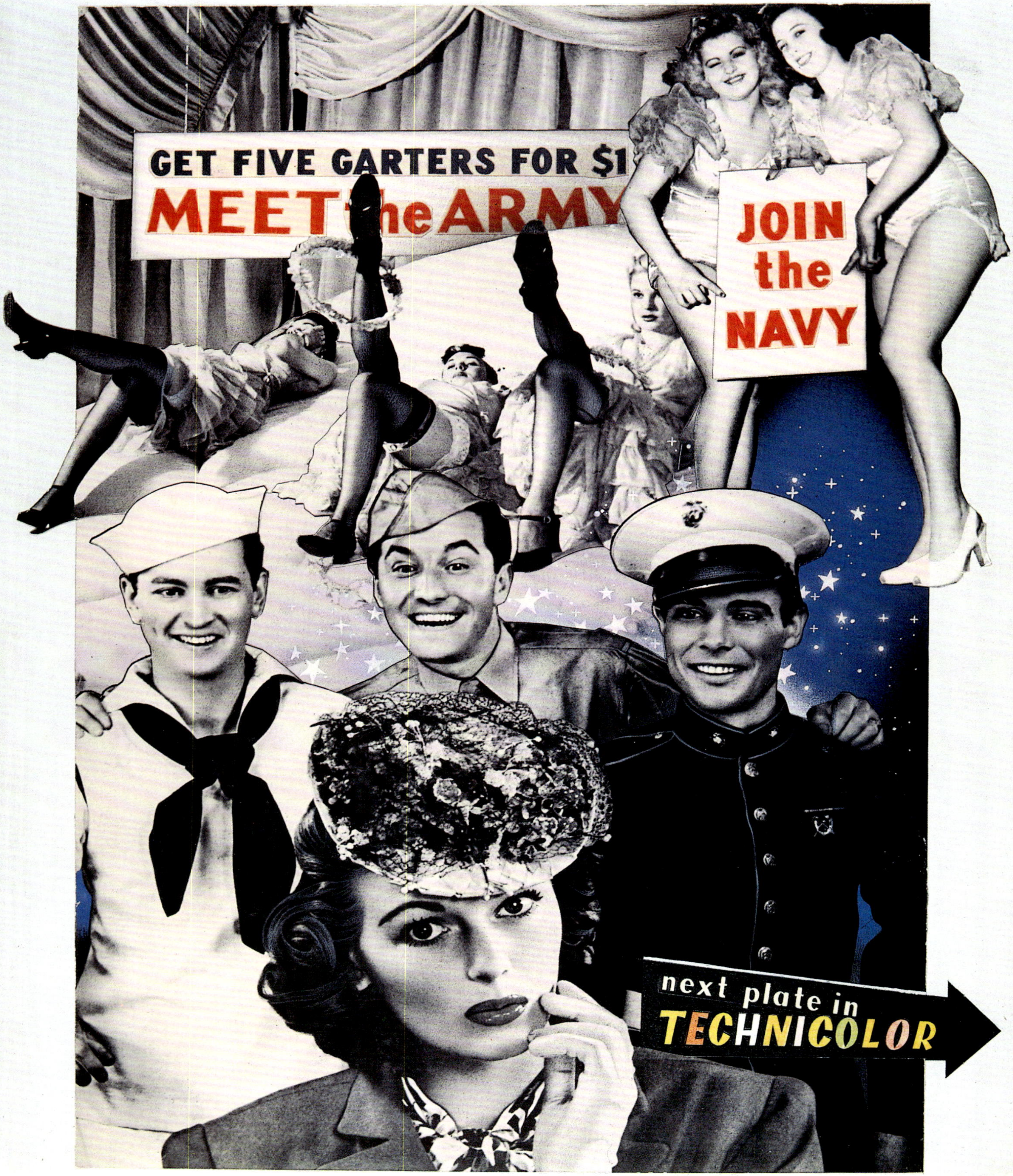


*Above and opposite*: Josep Renau, *Ah! Qué bella es la guerra. . . !* (Oh! This wonderful war. . . !), #34 from the series "The American Way of Life," Mexico, 1957

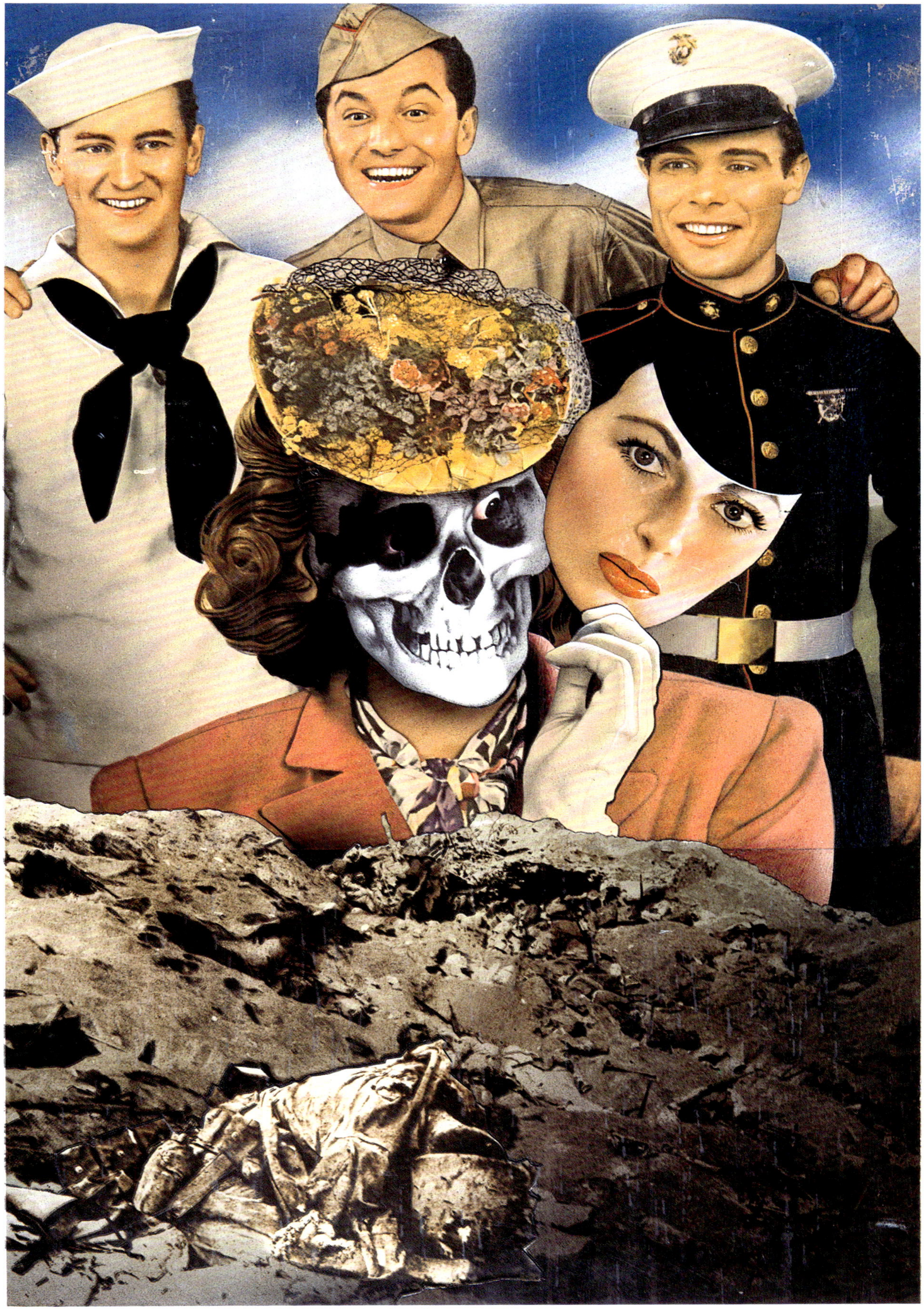

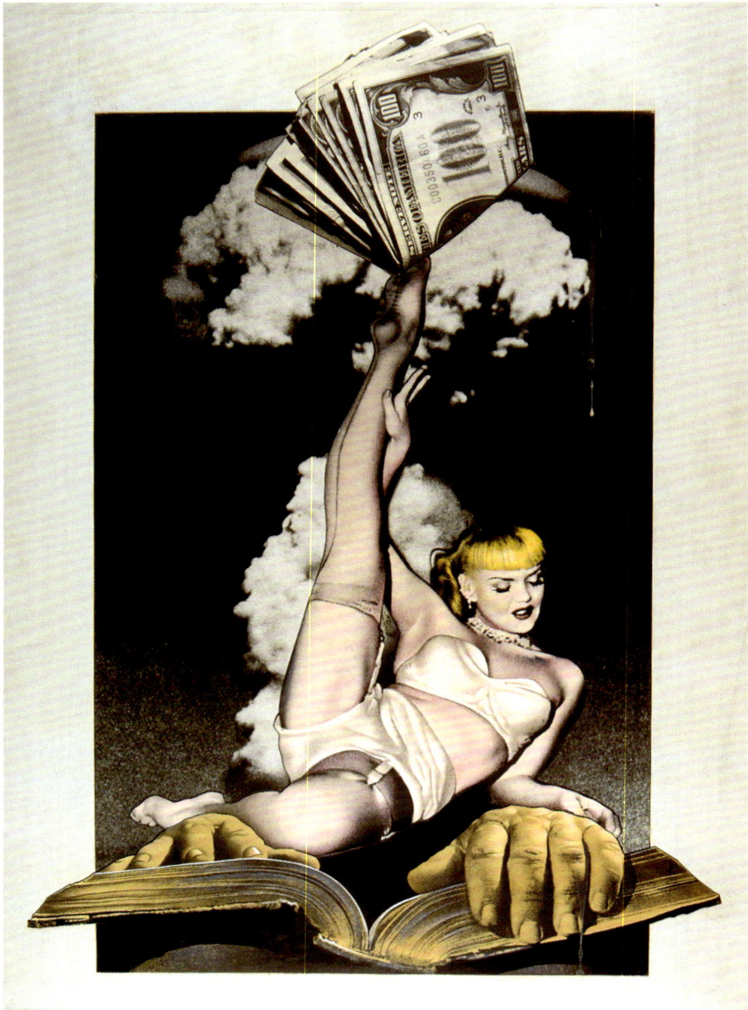

Josep Renau, *Equilibri* (Balance), #55 from the series
"The American Way of Life," Mexico, 1959

and product. A language invented with consumerist and alienating ends in mind was thus critically subverted. Renau's sources for the work were images that had appeared in *Life*, *Fortune*, and the *New York Times*, mouthpieces a priori of the slogans of peace, justice, well-being, and freedom that decorated the programs of their bosses. But Renau wanted to unveil the double face of these hypocritical and self-satisfied images, and to uncover the cost of their deceit: the repression, racism, corruption, speculation, militarization, and increasing arms production of a savage imperialism. The compositions often include quotes from the speeches of political leaders and public figures, or publicity slogans flagrantly contradicting the evidence shown in the pictures: the mushroom cloud over Hiroshima, the execution of Harold and Ethel Rosenberg, Ku Klux Klan lynchings, the commercial utilization of sex. Marilyn Monroe's dazzling smile was set next to images of deprived minorities, a hot dog next to an electric chair. Death in Renau's vision is the flip side of capitalist benefit.

"The American Way of Life" cycle anticipates some of the proposals of pop art: a realism that takes mass culture as its visual model, a tendency toward flashy iconography, an irony about consumerist myths, and a great visual clarity. The work can also be linked to creative photography of the time: it is interesting, for example, to see how these photomontages agree in some ways with the disillusioned and cynical vision of Robert Frank. But Frank's refined and sophisticated innovations in *The Americans* were not understood outside a limited elite of connoisseurs, while Renau took a much more belligerent and populist position. None of his photomontages is signed, and many have circulated anonymously, often outside his control. His goal was to plant in the minds of spectators, of whatever social rank and whatever cultural level, a direct and overwhelming message.

The mechanism by which the photomontages gain their significance can be studied on different levels. Where Heartfield's work, for instance, is based on juxtaposing elements that are contradictory or absurd, Renau's compositions are more dense and baroque, and, to catalyze spectators' reactions, often use metaphors that are as clearly understandable as they are grotesque. This grotesquerie—in contrast to Heartfield's gravity—Renau may have learned from the folklore of Valencia, its greatest manifestation being the *fallas*, huge bonfires set on St. John's Eve to consume *ninots*, papier-mâché dolls satirizing public personages or vices. The burlesque tone of these representations proves the abundance of stereotypes forged by popular creativity.

Renau sacrificed formal considerations to meaning, natural color to dramatic effect. The forced linkages and strident palette of the works were intended to heighten their impact. Concentrating on his message, the artist paid little attention to technical execution: he made no effort, for example, to hide the seams between the different graphic elements. Renau believed that the mere act of placing different images on the same plate forced the spectator to make connections between them. In contrast to many other photomontagists, he worked exclusively from found graphic materials, despite his own skill with a camera. Heartfield and Renau, who respected each other's ideological beliefs, kept up an interesting polemic regarding the plastic treatment of their respective styles. Renau, for example, argued that the chromatic austerity embraced by Heartfield was an antibourgeois necessity during the Weimar Republic, but that in an era dominated by the mass media and publicity, one had to fight the establishment with the new visual rhetoric imposed by the establishment itself.

In 1958, Renau went to the former East Germany, and in conceptual terms the corpus of "The American Way of Life" was finished. In Berlin, however, he continued to elaborate on the ideas he had worked out, until completing the more than 200 originals that made up the cycle. A selection of these photomontages was published for the first time in Berlin in 1967, under the title *Fata Morgana USA*. Today this assemblage of images remains the classical and definitive reference work of an art that, rather than just helping us to see the world, helps us to think of it critically in order to understand it and transform it.

Translated from the Spanish by Cola Franzen

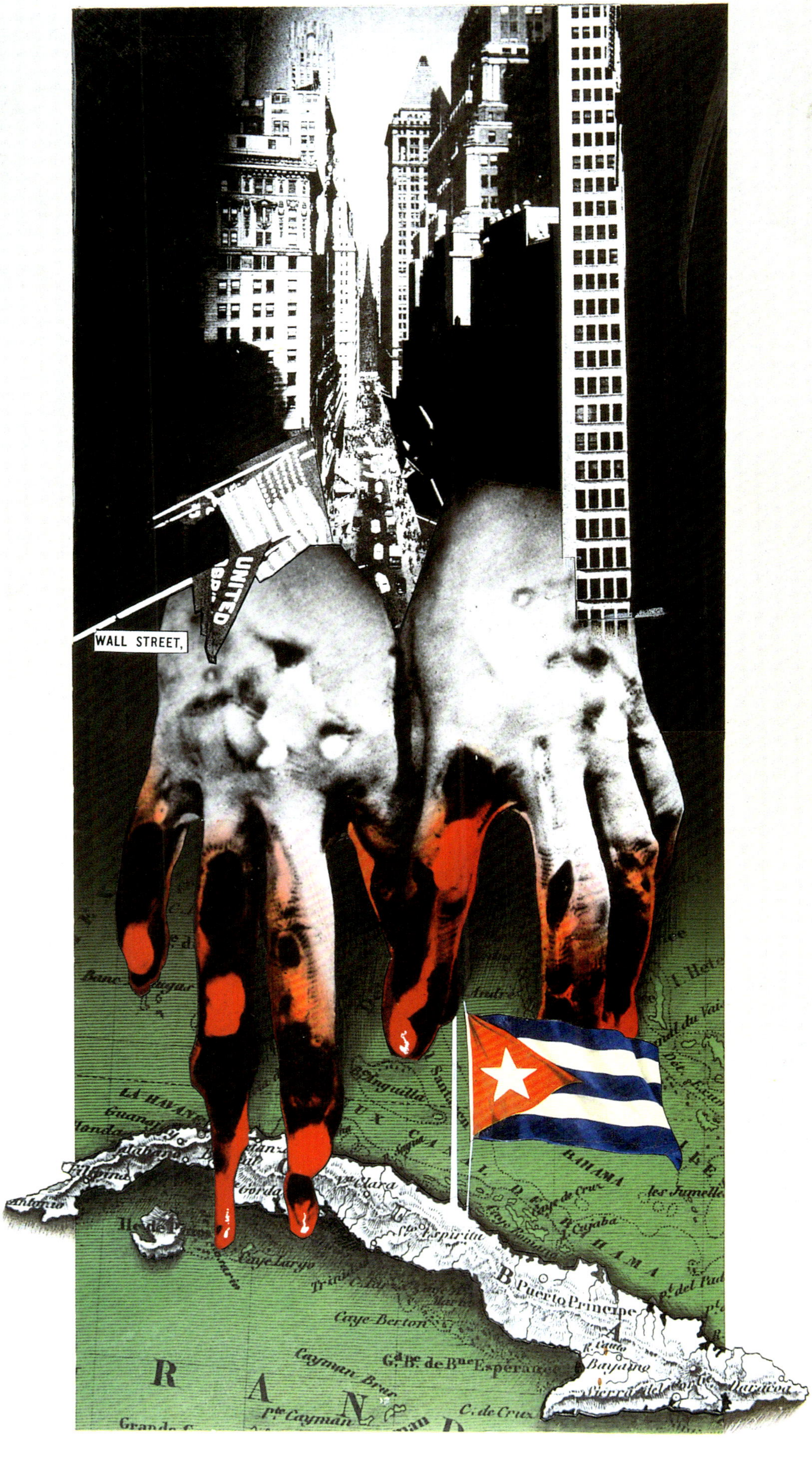


Josep Renau, *Fora les mans de Cuba!* (Hands off Cuba!), #61 from the series "The American Way of Life," Mexico, 1962

# THE PHOTOGRAPHS OF RAÚL CORRALES AND CONSTANTINO ARIAS

## By Alma Guillermoprieto

If we state that a photograph never portrays reality, but is rather an image of the dreamlike state induced in the photographer at the moment of his or her encounter with reality, *Cuba: Dos épocas* provides us with marvelous proof of our thesis. Constantino Arias, who created his best work in the period immediately before the watershed year of 1959, and Raúl Corrales, who came into his own as an artist thanks to Fidel Castro's revolution, present photographs that lead to a Cuban reverie because they are, in turn, images of two dreams.

According to what can be learned from books, Cuba is a sugar-producing nation of barely twelve million people. It is poor, like so many of its island neighbors, adrift in a sea barely large enough to act as a conduit between two continents. But the island of dreams that Constantino Arias shows us is another country altogether: it is the magical and exalted spot in which all the races and all the pleasures of the planet converge in an endless exhibitionist feast. It is a country of chorus girls, cabaret artists, gamblers, revelers, night owls, and bongo players, whose very sense of themselves depends on being able to display their salsa, their shimmy, their joy of life, and their behinds before our astonished and delighted eyes.

There was a time when Arias's photographs were used to demonstrate the abject decadence to which a succession of dictators had brought the Cuban people. Now that postrevolutionary Cuba, too, offers sun, booze, and whores to the dollar-carrying tourist, the same images lose their accusatory charge. Instead, they can usefully help explain why Cuba has always occupied a privileged spot in the world's collective dreamscape of pleasure.

A key can be found in a pair of portraits: one of a black couple, professional dancers of rumba who are not young, and who nevertheless show off their less-than-firm flesh with provocative cheer; the other of an extremely white-skinned blonde who, naked, examines herself in a mirror with delighted satisfaction. What sets Cuba apart even from other orgiastic cultures is that it has always offered pleasure without shame and without guilt—or, at least, this is the fantasy proposed in Arias's work, which so perfectly matches our own: in the Cuba of the permanent carnival, there are those who pay and those who buy, but the party is for everyone.

Three or four of Arias's photographs—a beggar outside a hospital, a woman in her squalid kitchen—help us see how it could have been possible for the pleasure-loving Cubans to surrender wholly to the ascetic Fidel Castro. But the fact is that there is no satisfactory explanation for a revolution. What Raúl Corrales's photographs manage to do is submerge us in the revolutionary fantasy that captivated an entire idealistic generation worldwide. Here are the bearded rebels—*los barbudos*—the enraptured followers of el Barbudo Mayor, Fidel. Here is Fidel himself, heroic in the wilderness of the Sierra Maestra. Here is the New Man, hacking his way through the underbrush.

Corrales's most hypnotic photographs breathe the humidity of the tropical countryside—rebels with rain, rebels with mountains, rebels against a backdrop of storm clouds. It is worth remembering that the thousand and one rural guerrilla groups that sprang up all over the world in the wake of the Sierra Maestra epic were largely the creation of urban youths, virgins in their experience with the tropical wild, who felt they had to go in search of a sacred mystery at its heart. Throughout the years that this revolutionary impulse lasted, the clandestine operatives in the cities consistently took more losses and were tortured and imprisoned in greater numbers than their rural counterparts, yet the rebels in the mountains and the jungle were always the ones who enjoyed greater moral authority—as if communion with nature were indeed the act that would lead humanity to that higher stage dreamed of by Che Guevara.

The magnetic pull of the guerrillas' bucolic utopia was so strong that, after the Revolution's triumph, Fidel realized that he would have to return to the Sierra Maestra with his former combatants so that Corrales could take some of the more emblematic pictures in this book. In other words, the pictures of the *barbudos* in the

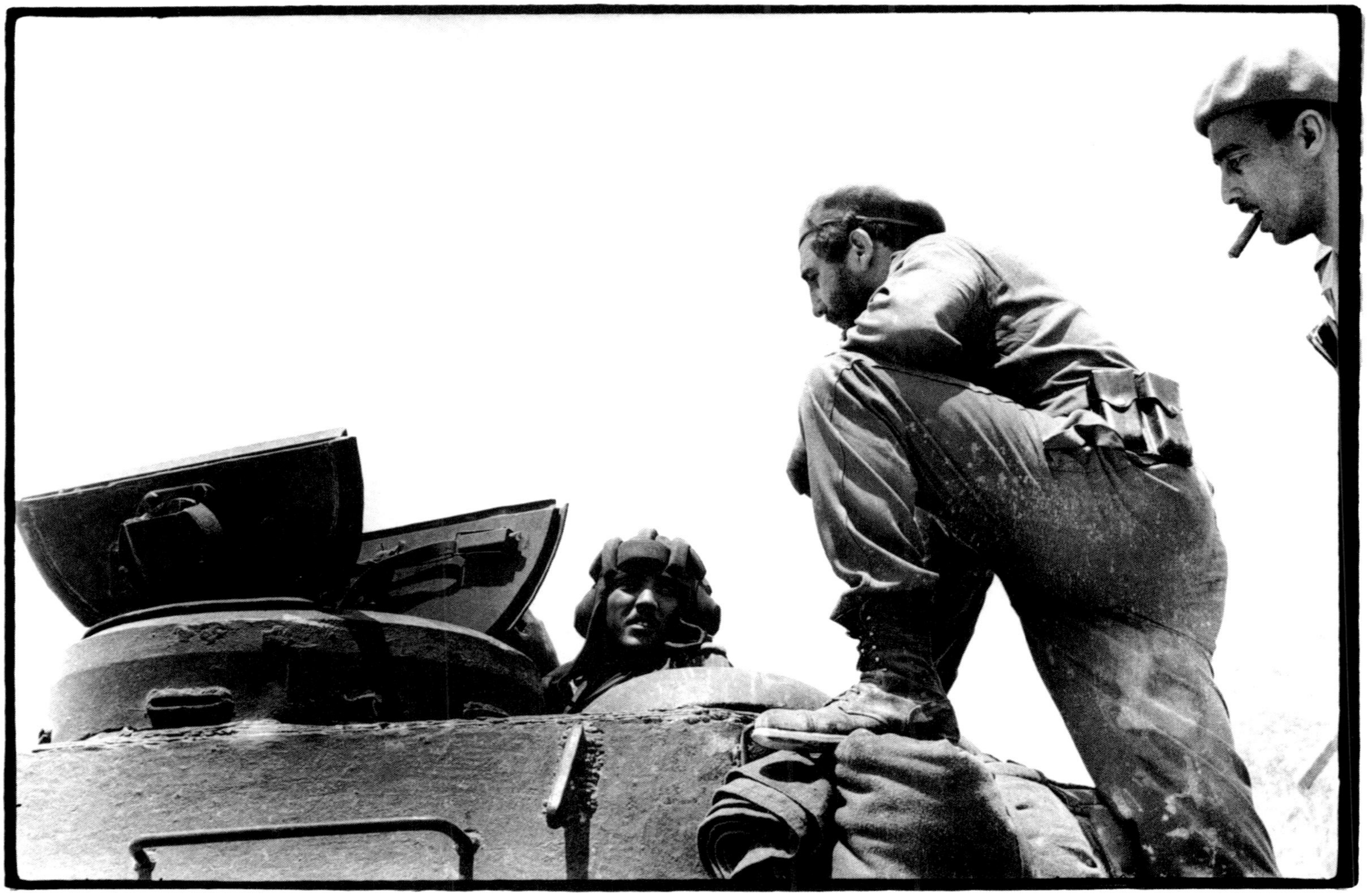

Raúl Corrales, *Fidel Castro en Playa Girón* (Fidel Castro at Girón Beach), Cuba, 1961

woods are staged. But it doesn't matter. We still want to see them, so we can dream again, like in the old days.

There are also "real" photographs, so to speak. In one, militiamen prepare their defense against the coming invasion from the north with the help of some toy planes; in another, young soldiers from the brand-new Cuban Revolutionary Armed Forces celebrate their wedding under an arch formed by antiaircraft guns. Oddly, it is these unstaged pictures that cut most uncomfortably close to the rhetorical. The Revolution allowed Corrales to live off his work as a recognized artist; in exchange, he lost the unpretentious self-confidence of the artisan, which is one of the qualities that makes Arias's work so beguiling. But Corrales's achievement is part of history; he captured the moment when Cuba stopped displaying itself for others and turned its full attention inward. None of his images is marked by the compulsive need to please that appears again and again in Arias's most distinctive work. In Corrales's portrait of a rebel napping in a bourgeois residence, we are once again seduced by the sensuality and beauty of the Cuban people, but this time we also feel relief, because the photograph's subject doesn't seem interested in us in the slightest. Soon, the Revolution would turn its attention to the creation of an image of Cuba worthy of feeding the world's dreams. (Corrales's staged photographs in the Sierra Maestra are a beginning.) But in these first, fresh images of the Revolution, the world is new, and so is our gaze.

Translated from Spanish

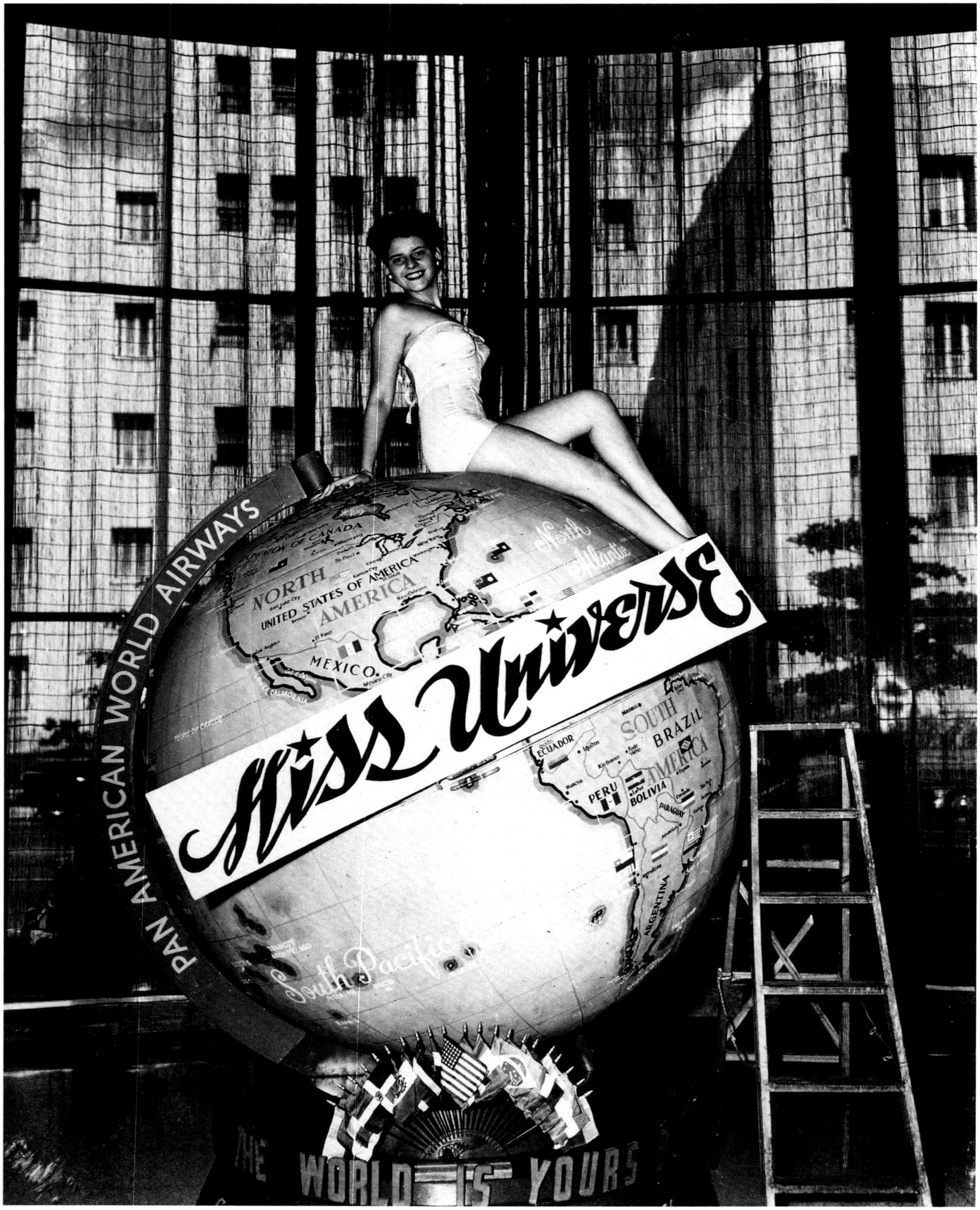
PAN AMERICAN WORLD AIRWAYS
Miss Universe
THE WORLD IS YOURS

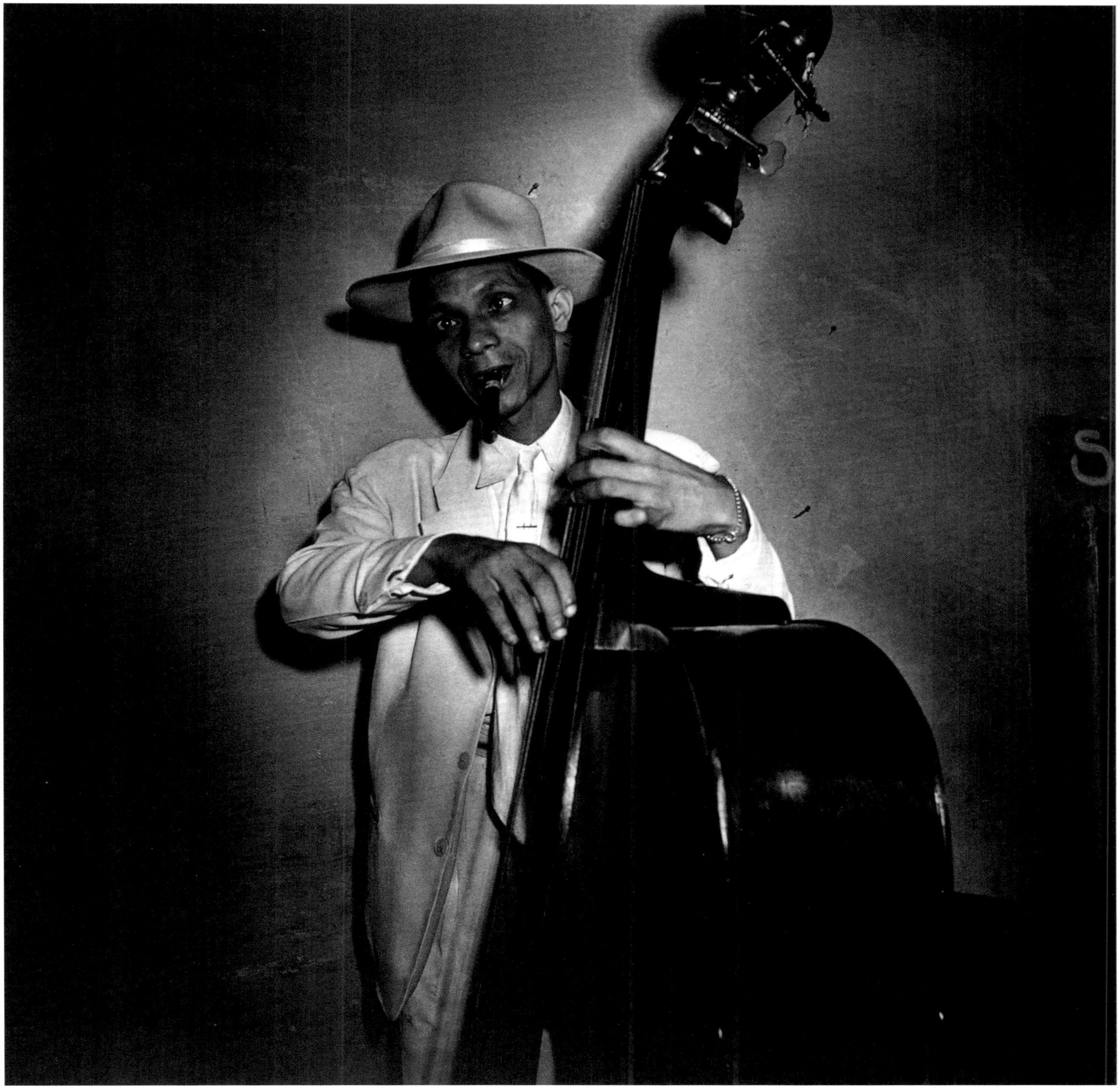

Constantino Arias, *El bizco* (The cross-eyed man),
Rumba Palace, Havana, Cuba, 1950

*Opposite*: Constantino Arias, *Miss Universo* (Miss Universe),
Havana, Cuba, 1950

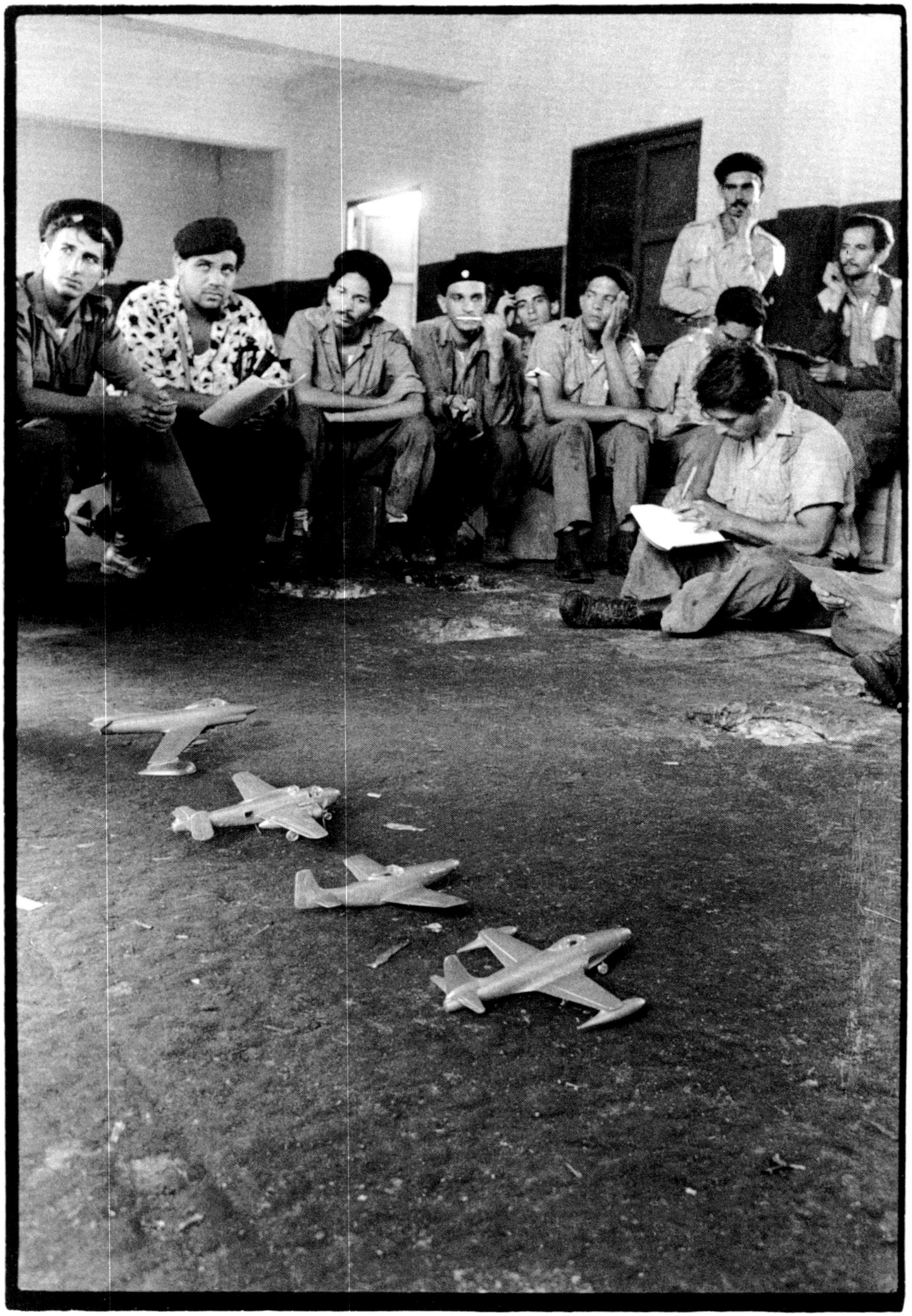

Raúl Corrales, *Defensa antiaérea* (Antiaircraft defense), Cuba, 1960

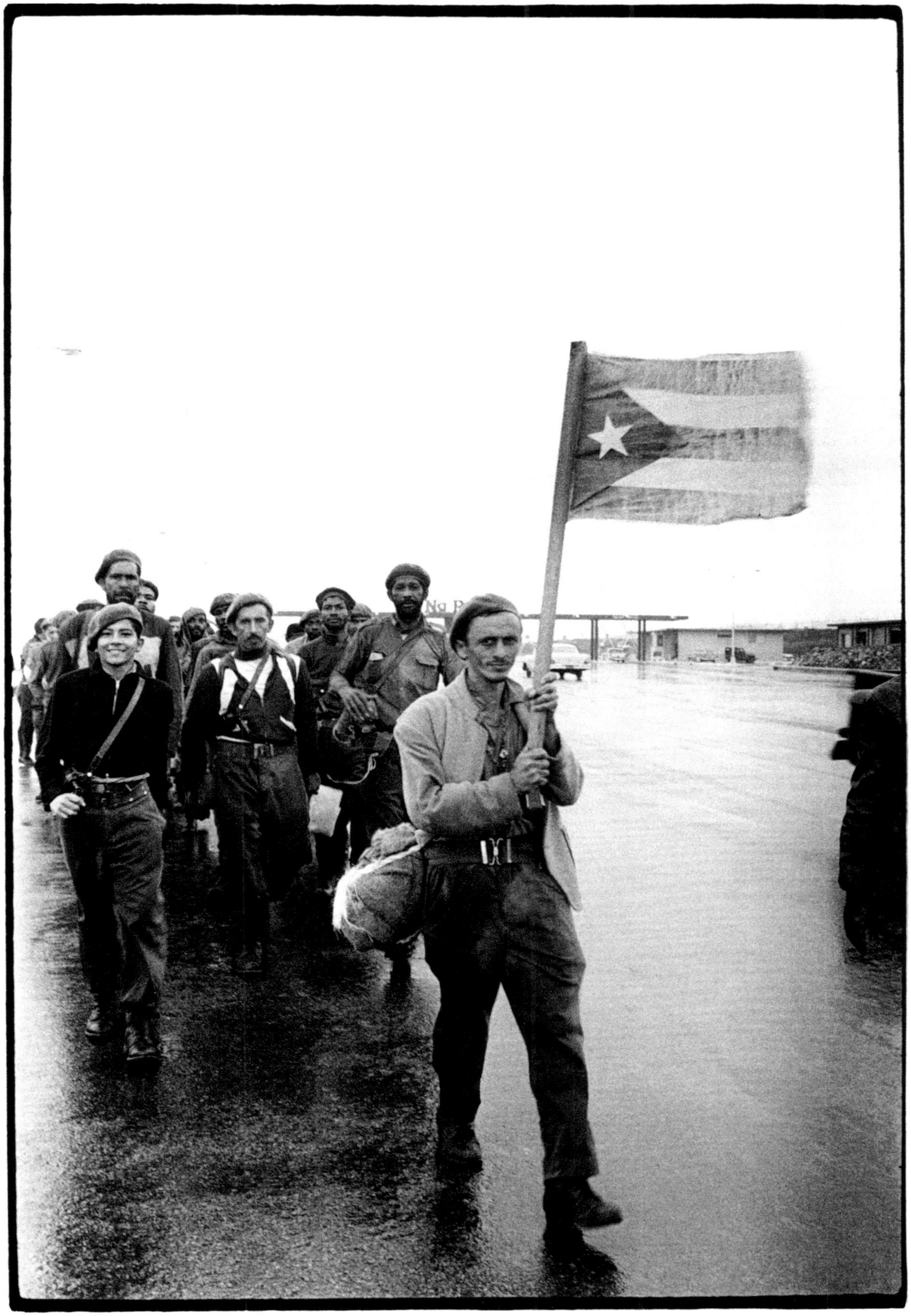

Raúl Corrales, *Salida de La Habana* (Leaving Havana), Cuba, January 1961

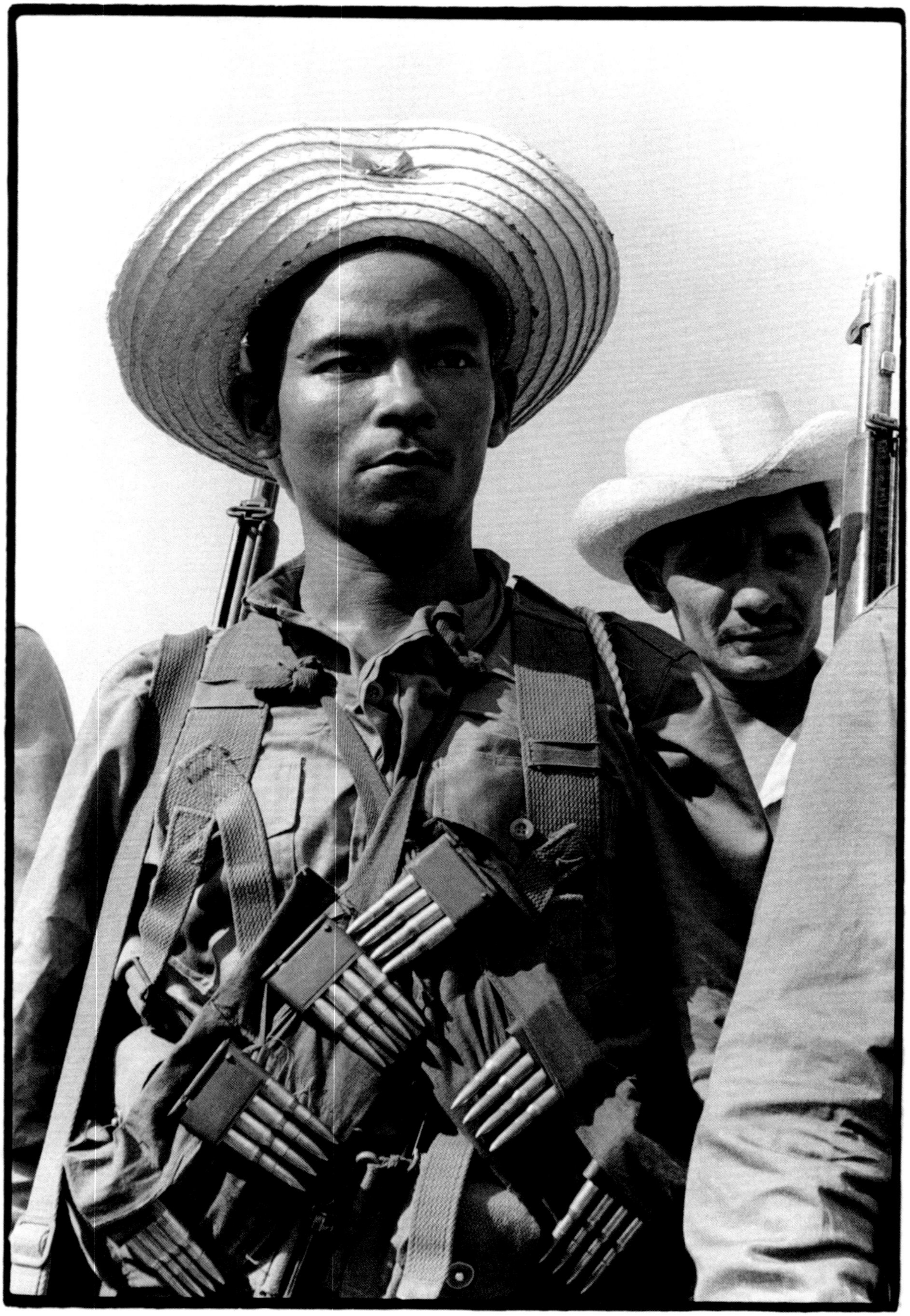

Raúl Corrales, *Bandoleras* (Soldiers wearing bandoliers), Llanos de Oriente, Cuba, 1959

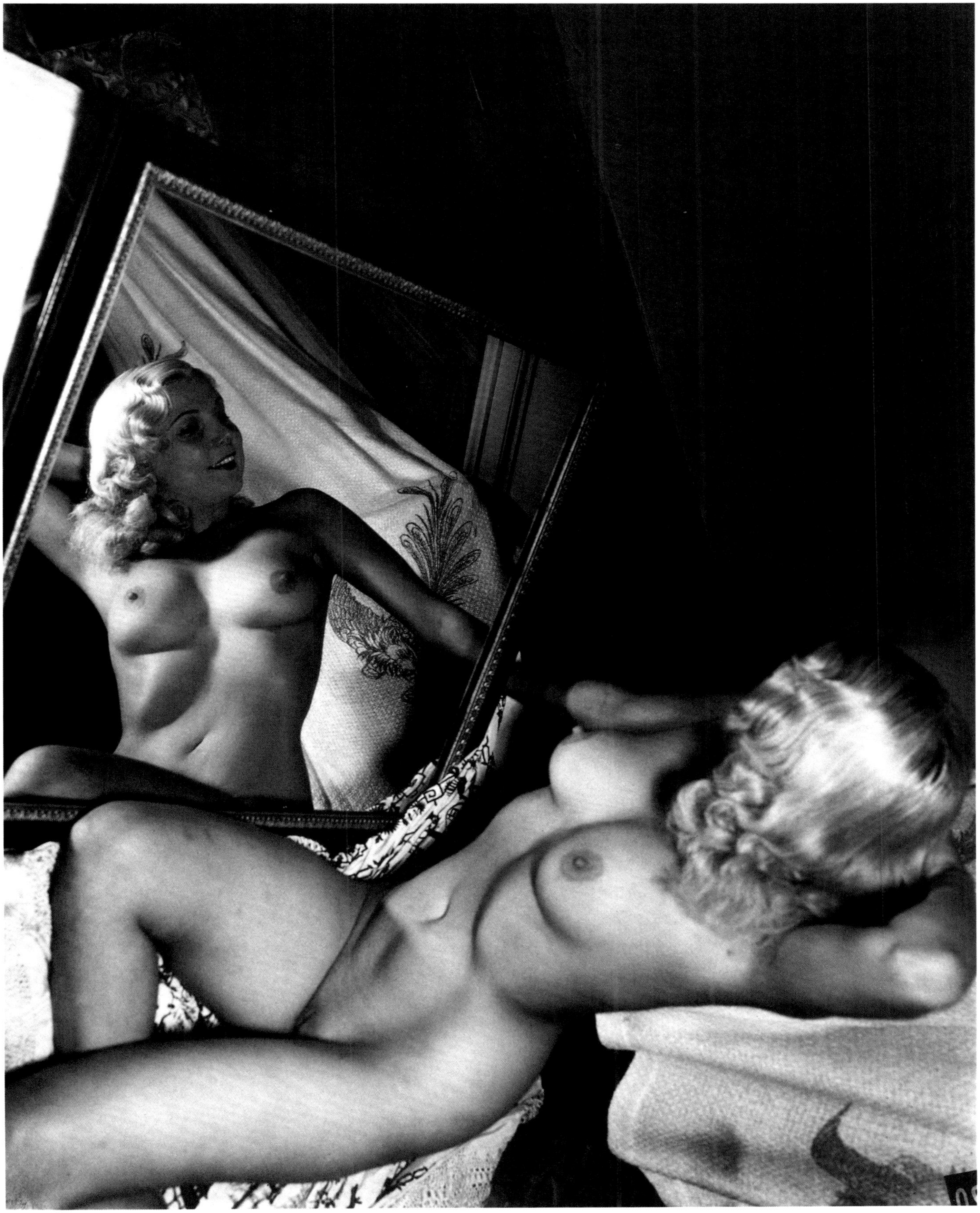

Constantino Arias, *Leda frente al espejo* (Leda in front of the mirror), Havana, Cuba, 1949

# The Fifties

## BEFORE THE FLOOD: NACHO LÓPEZ AND HÉCTOR GARCÍA

### By Carlos Monsiváis

Appreciation for the artistic dimensions of photography is a recent phenomenon in Mexico: as late as the 1970s, the usual thing was to applaud the technological miracle and leave it at that, reserving all astonishment for the invention itself. And if photography was only occasionally considered art, the kind of photography destined for immediate publication—photojournalism—was seen as having only one clear merit, that of being a gift of opportunity. This delay in acknowledging an artistic discipline explains why two great photographers, Nacho López and Héctor García, were for so long considered merely visual reporters, no doubt excellent in their way but hardly creators. The quality of the reproduction of their work was not even minimally acceptable, and no public existed with an eye schooled enough to admire their talent.

Unconcerned by this lack of appreciation, López and García made full use of certain qualities of the journalist's métier: exceptional situations, the need to sum up a broad phenomenon in a single image, and the pressure of circumstances, which, in conjunction with a critical temperament, can refine one's point of view. To all of this, both photographers added the lessons of their inevitable teacher, Manuel Álvarez Bravo, from whom they learned something indispensable in a country like Mexico: an aesthetic perspective in which attention is paid not to the prestige or status of the subject matter, but to what is disdained or barely noticed, to what can only be unlocked by the keys of poetry, be it a woman combing her hair reinvented by the light, or the halo of blood around a murdered workman.

Álvarez Bravo's teachings ran deep with López and García, but his disciples aimed for lyrical exaltation in only a part of their work. Some of their photographs can undoubtedly be called poetic, but that quality was not their habitual target. Instead they focused on another zone of the aesthetic, one that derives its energy from a great city that neither entirely abandons tradition nor fully joins with modernity. What these photographers found in the megalopolis—in the ebb and flow of the streets, the constant new environments—certainly can be poetic but is more often something only definable by photography itself: the photographic event that incorporates violence and politics and entertainment and sexual appetite and the bedazzlement of the senses. At the center of López and García's interest was the artistic expressiveness to be found in documenting city life.

Nacho López was born in Tampico, Tamaulipas in 1924, and died in Mexico City in 1986. He started out taking color photos for magazines and newspapers. His inventiveness was extraordinary: he was the first person in Mexico to create photographic series, extending individual visual discoveries into memorable stories. The figures in López's series are symbolic precisely because of their singular character, from the very attractive young woman who is followed in her walk down the street, with an admiration that amounts to a sexual imprisonment, to the young man carrying a mannequin into a *pulquería*. López's originality was such that for a long time his work was called "picturesque," which it certainly is not—such was the prevailing ignorance. López was not an amusing eccentric; his lack of visual prejudice allowed him to glimpse another, emergent urban landscape. And his contribution was significant enough to remain untouched by the deluge of imitations and plagiarisms. López observes the new urban life with great acuity, and, as he wrote in 1964, he acquaints us with "I, the citizen," the resident of the beautiful, and universal, city.

López's photographs are symbolic only insofar as reality continues to reproduce them today (the symbol being that which is never exhausted, because another similar image always perpetuates it): the boys trying out their boxing skills in the street, the prisoner in the precinct house, the orator at the protest meeting, a stretch of down time at work, the children undimmed by wretched

Nacho López, *Calle Ejido* (Ejido Street), Mexico City, Mexico, ca. 1958

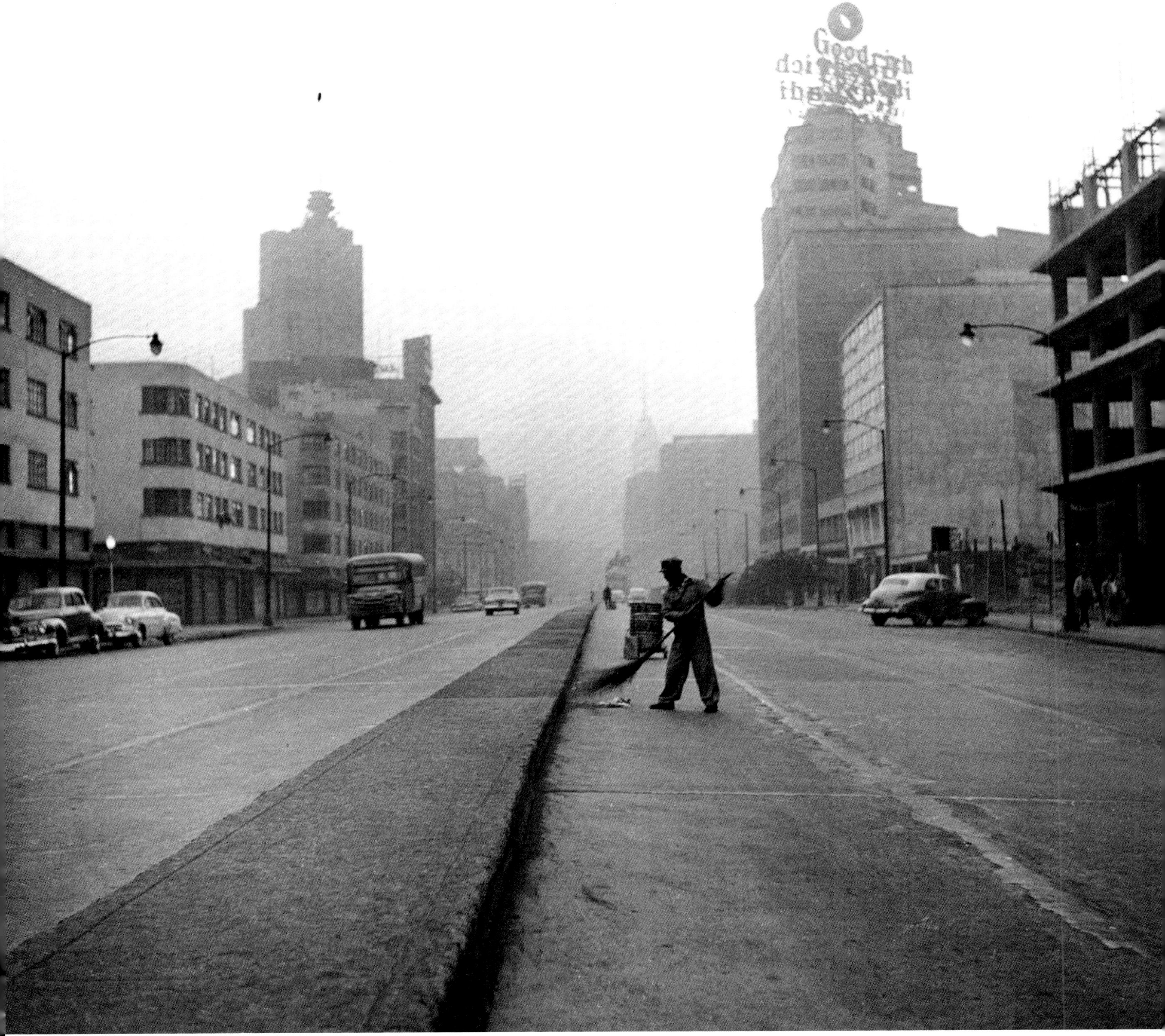
Goodrich

poverty, the crowd yearning for whatever it is that will be extinguished as soon as it disperses, the vedette in the sleazebag cabaret, the women gnawed by worry. Occasionally a photograph appears that defies all explanations and foreseeable contexts: the hands of a prisoner sticking out from beneath a cell door, a magnificent sunset over a city with a monstrous mixture of periods and styles. The image generally derives not from a quest for poetic moments but from the repertory of chance.

López handles the countryside equally well, documenting indigenous customs, proud and laughing faces, dramatic moments, rituals, and a poetry in one place unexpected, in another always a presence. His pictures of the city, though, may be his greatest contribution. Here his obsessions are dispersed across the statements and restatements of the great city—the faith that gazes unsparingly at modernity, chaos, merriment, protest, sex, solitude, drunkenness. His images say, "The nights, violent or serene, soaked with blood, alcohol, and marijuana, repeat their stories: the will to die and the same eternal passion, deceit, and crime." In Nacho López's work the great city is an unfulfilled prophecy, an unexpected revelation, as close to festive delirium as to nightmare.

Héctor García was born in Mexico City in 1926. Like López, he began as a photojournalist, and refined his practice in that occupation; unlike López, he plunged wholeheartedly into journalism, which made it possible for him to travel and to bear witness to a wide variety of scenes and privileged moments, and ensured that a range of reactions to extreme events was always available to him. If García's work recalls anything in this respect, it is the work of the U.S. photographer Weegee, a devotee of crime scenes and the flow of urban contrasts. García focuses on what the city and his work as a journalist demand of him, lying in wait not for the poetic moment but for the unexpected—or expected—image that a highly trained eye can capture instantaneously.

The artist David Alfaro Siqueiros, jailed as a "subversive," appears in García's work, accepting the photographer's request to pose as a figure in one of his own huge paintings. Here we also find the painter Diego Rivera in his studio, his smile rivaling the smile of an enormous cardboard doll; a lady at a gala dinner, bending down to straighten her dress; some isolated rifles lying in the Plaza de las Tres Culturas on October 2, 1968, the day of a student massacre; a cat in New York, with a lonely-looking house in the background; a woman at a reception who bows as a diplomat studies her neckline. García also photographs endless street scenes, ceremonies of all kinds, writers, crowds both angry and festive, artists, urban anecdotes. The catalog is vast.

García's work as a journalist also sends him into the countryside; his series on the Huichol Indians, with their hallucinatory rituals and wanderings, is magnificent, as is his series on Oaxaca. But the fundamental element in this work is the tendency of a forced modernization to bring on poverty and overcrowding—not a timeless poverty, either, but a specifically contemporary one in its greed and shamelessness. Yet García's heroes and antiheroes have an ease and vitality. His knowing combination of tradition and unforeseen incident makes the photographs memorable; García brings to his intrusions into people's lives, his strolls through the city, an honest desire to surprise himself. An example: on a street in a poor neighborhood, a boy, in a niche for a missing saint, makes an obscene gesture at the photographer and whoever else is around. The opposite can also take place: an indigenous girl covers herself with her rebozo, leaving nothing but a single eye free to interrogate the outer world.

In the street, his native territory, Héctor García works with imagination and rigor. The asphalt jungle belongs to him, and he penetrates its enigmas without trying to impress or shock. What matters to him is grace, cynicism, vigor, the tenderness of daily life, which social disdain renders invisible but which art recovers, with feeling and irony.

Translated from the Spanish by Esther Allen

Héctor García, *Niño en el vientre de concreto*
(Child in a concrete belly), Mexico City, Mexico, 1952

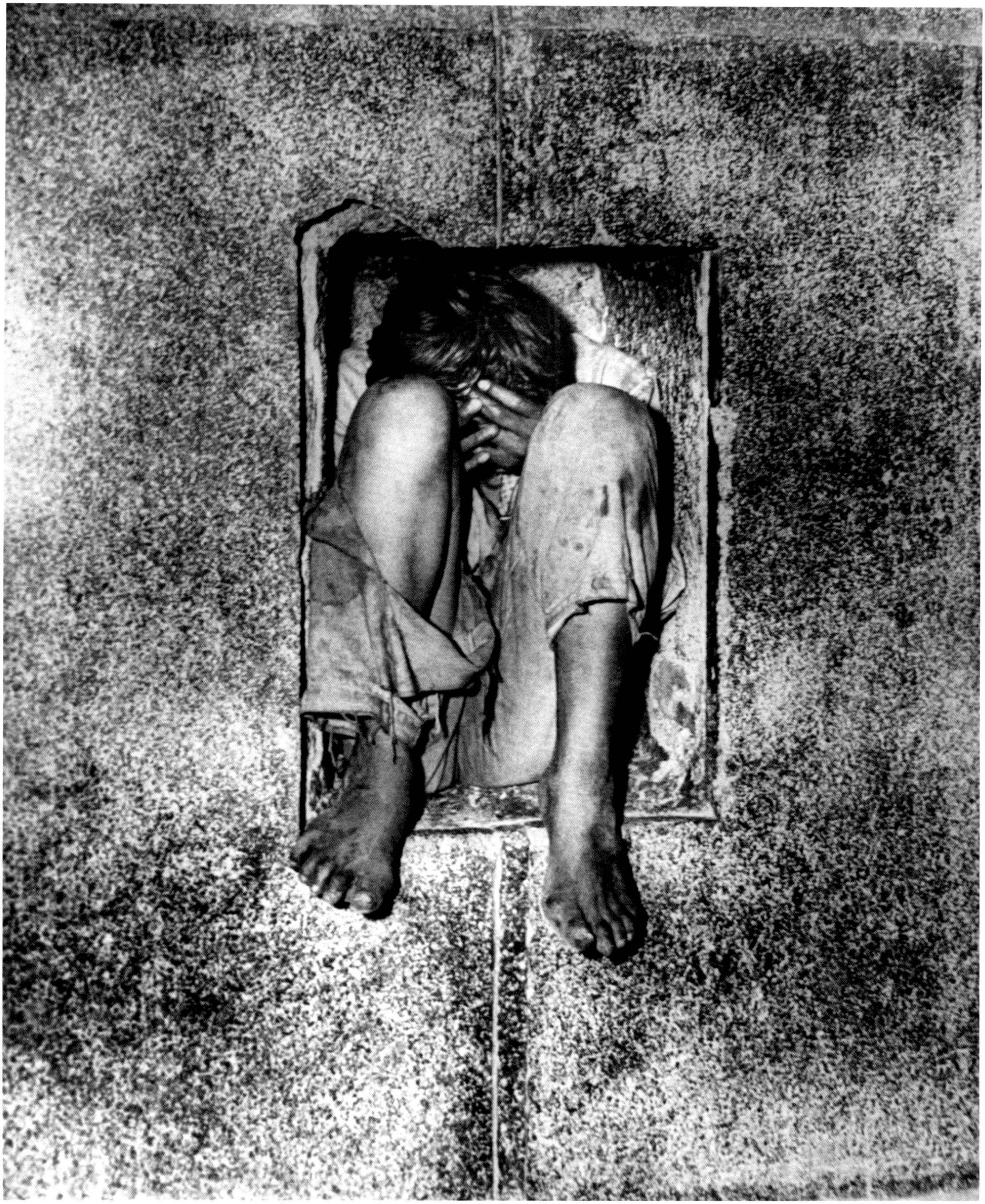

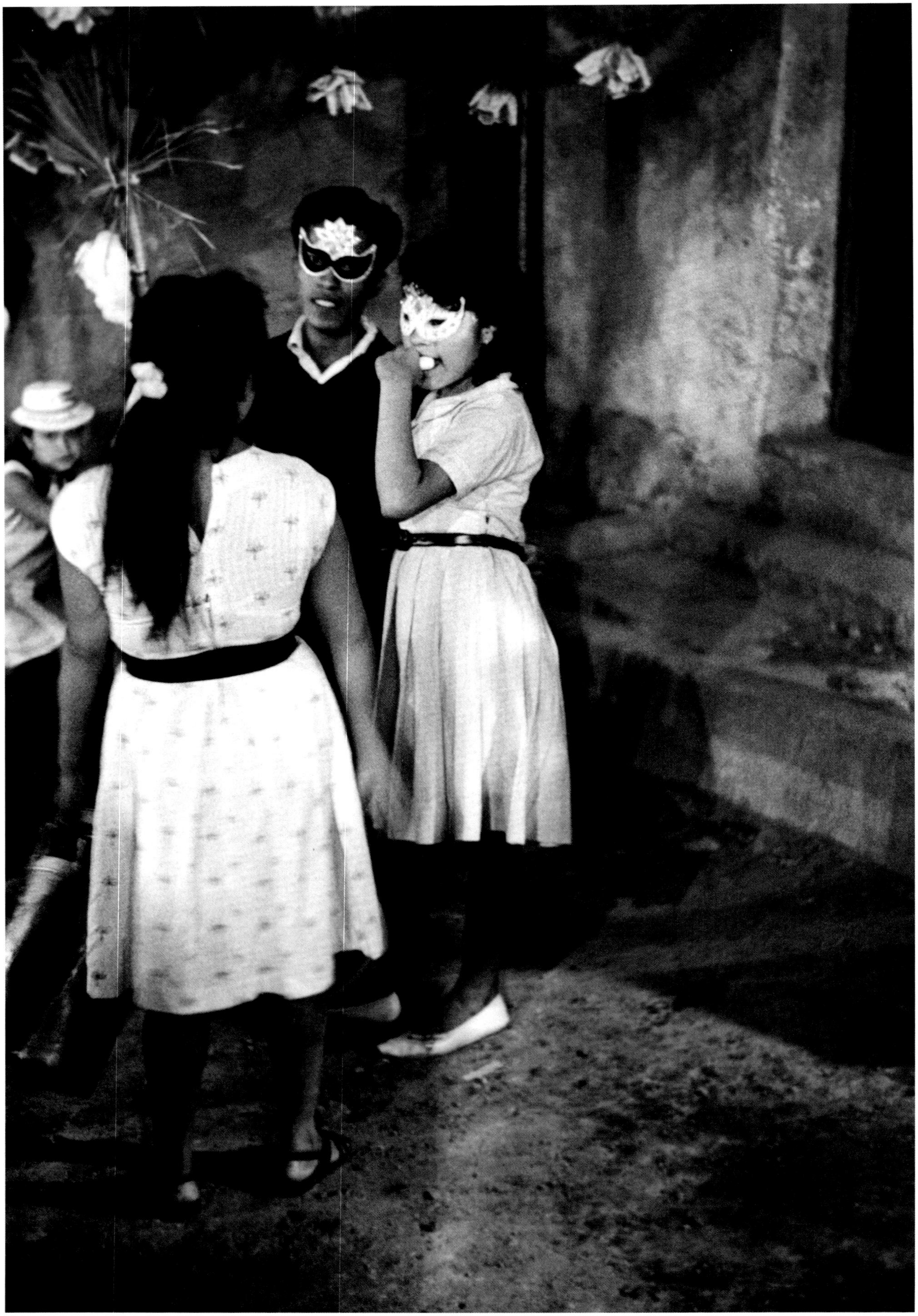

Nacho López, *Carnaval en Cuernavaca* (Carnival in Cuernavaca), Morelos, Mexico, 1970

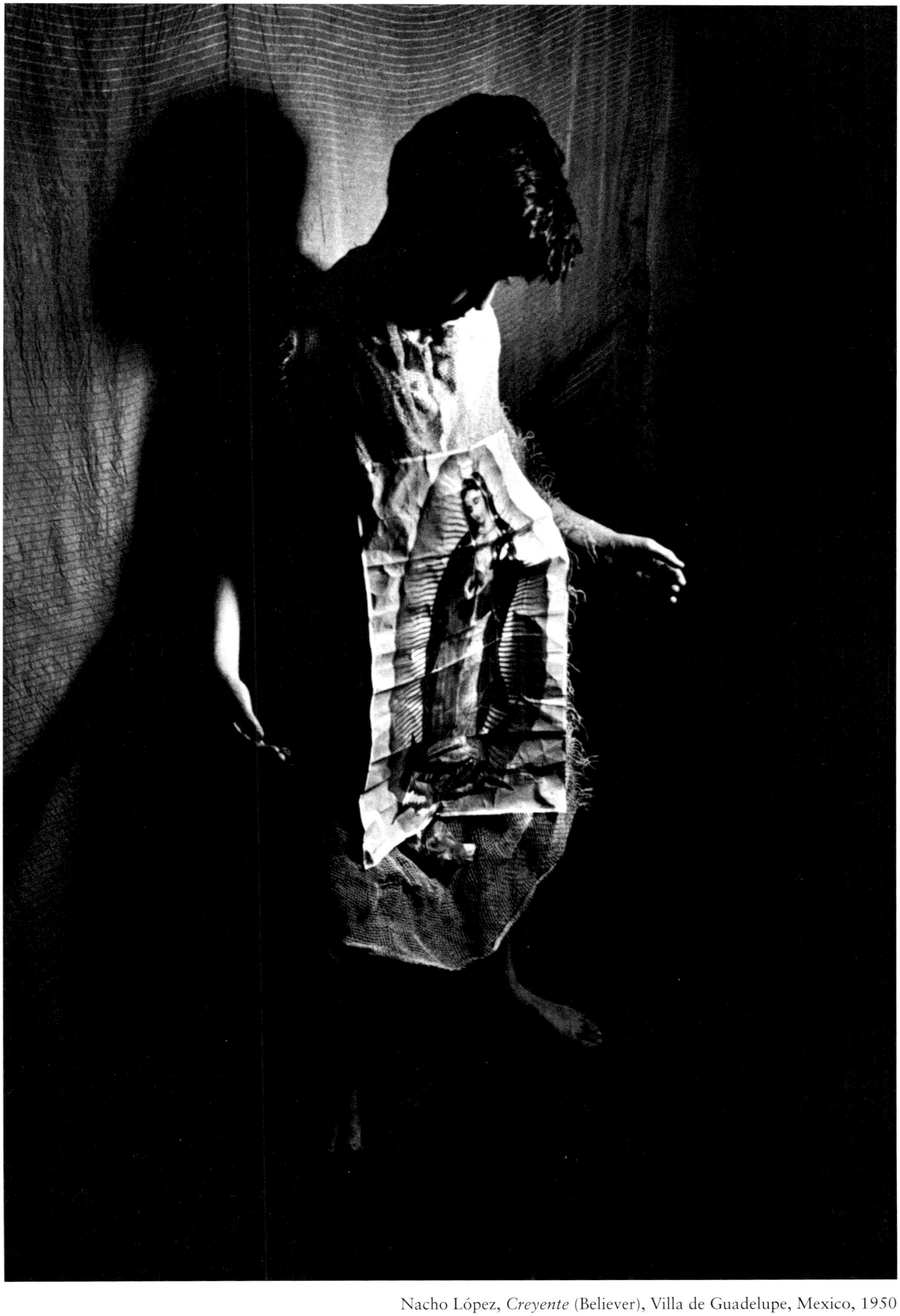

Nacho López, *Creyente* (Believer), Villa de Guadelupe, Mexico, 1950

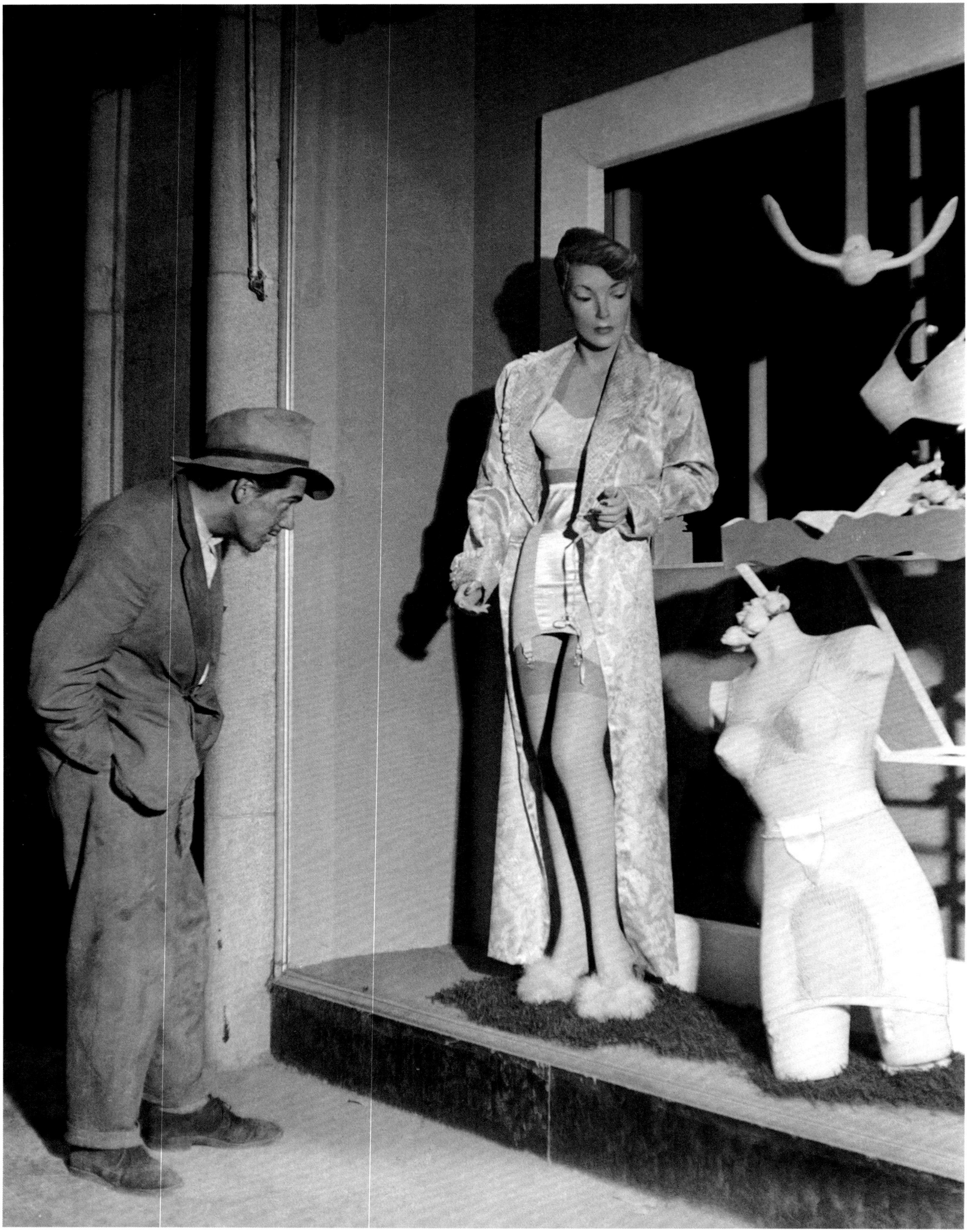

Héctor García, *Ventana de las ansias* (Window of yearnings), Mexico City, Mexico, 1949

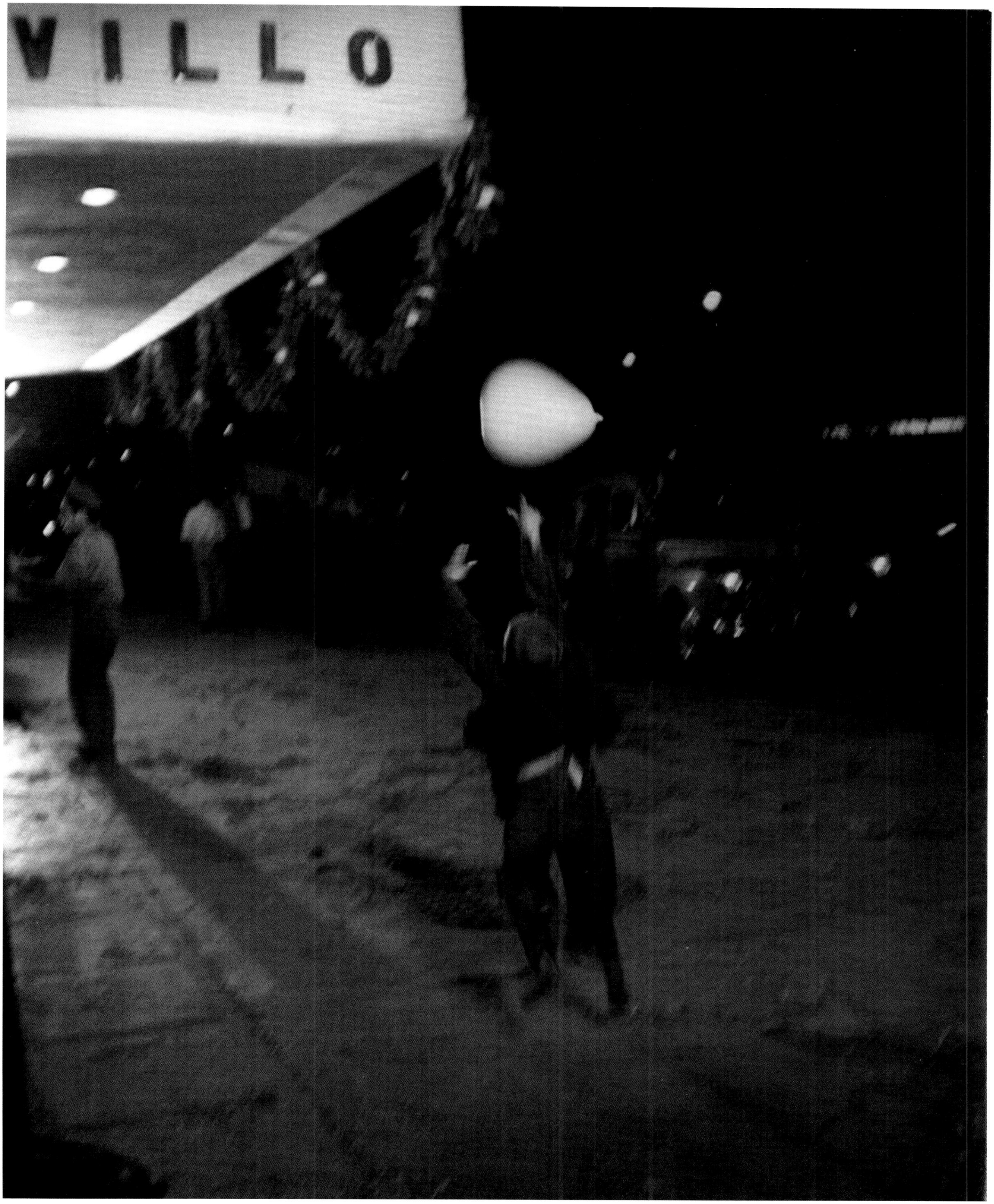


Héctor García, *Prometeo* (Prometheus), Mexico City, Mexico, ca. 1940

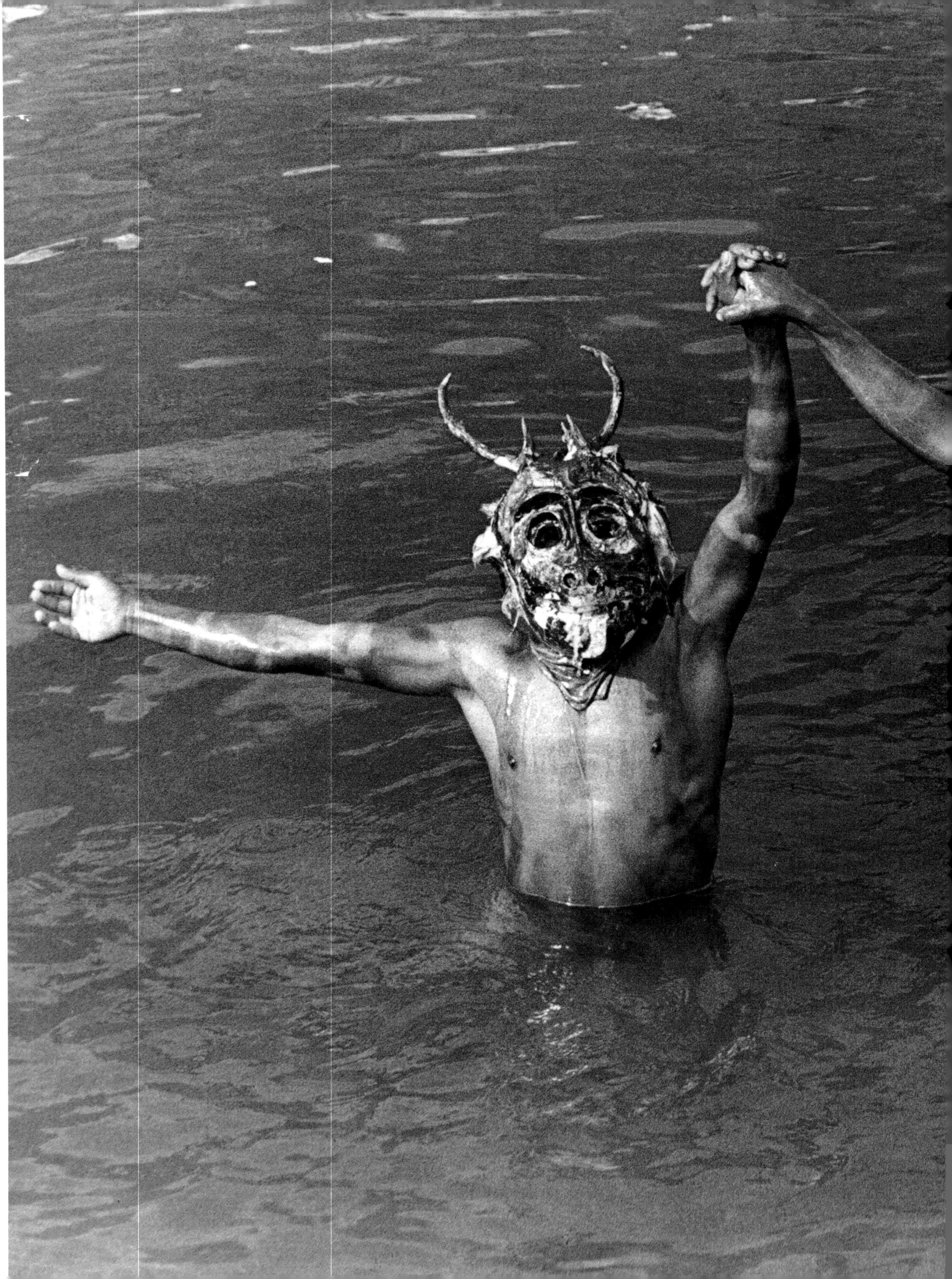

Héctor García, *Sábado de Gloria Cora* (Saturday of glory among the Coras), Nayarit, Mexico, 1969

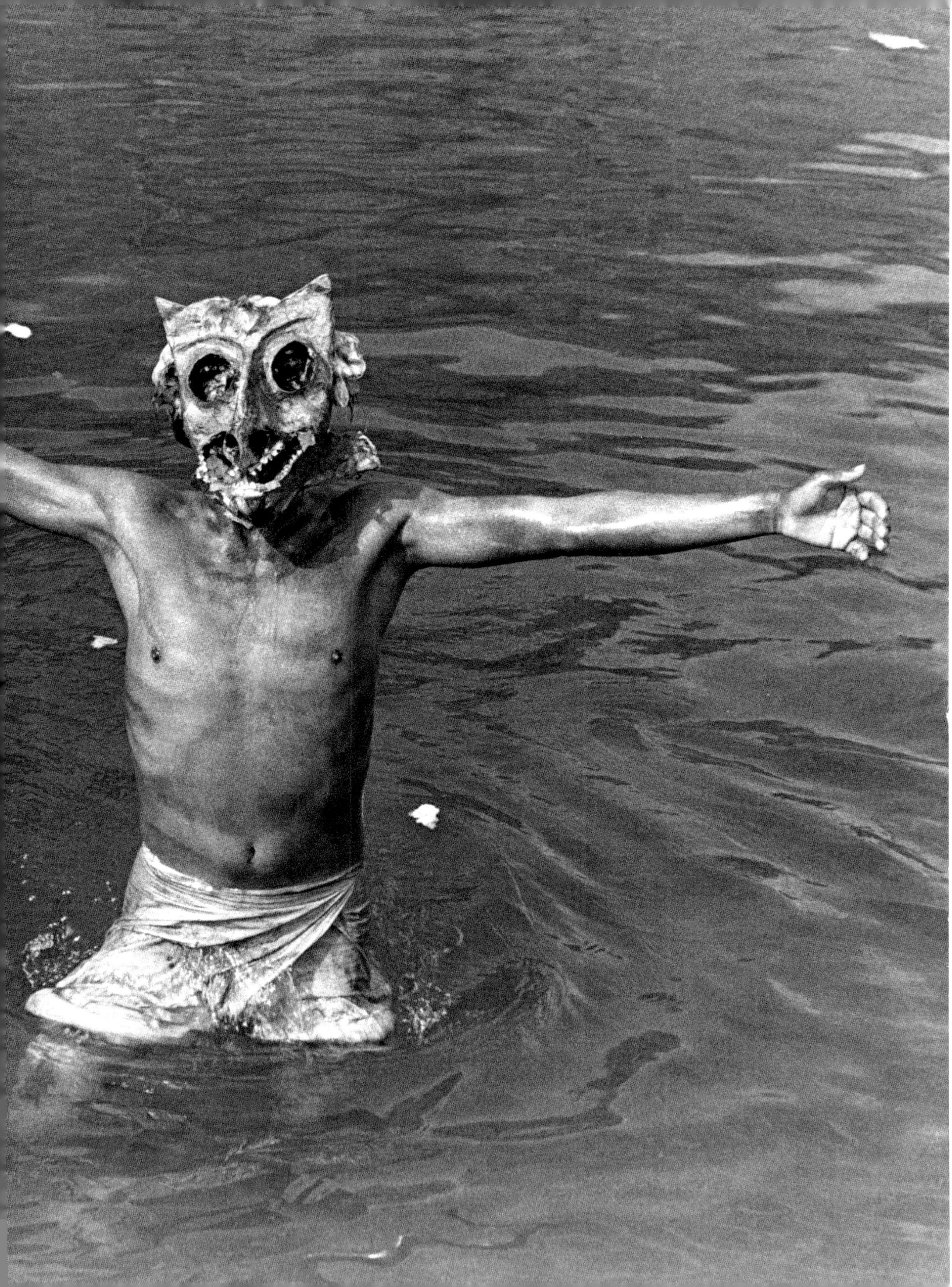

# Poetry of the Onlooker

## THE EYE'S DOMAIN

### By Verónica Volkow

Photographers are wanderers, travelers, and explorers, searching—in the deserts, the villages, on the roads, in people's faces—for the poetic image, the image that freezes us in time, that suspends our scrutiny of something outside us and starts us questioning what is within, that starts us seeing in a new way. Every true journey on which a photographer takes us sets off in two directions: outward, to watch the fast-moving strip of surprises along the road—faces, landscapes, streets—and inward, into the impelling flow of the internal monologue. It is a journey that always exposes us to the unknown, renewing our inquiry. The constant nearness of the unforeseen to which it exposes us awakens our senses, increasing the eagerness with which we see, limbering the muscles of the imagination. The being that we are in relation to space seems to grow larger as it takes in other colors, other forms, other connections; and as a result, we seem radically to rethink what, under unfamiliar conditions and perspectives, we might be. That is perhaps the true passion of the journey constituted by the photograph: witnessing the advent of a new, revitalized inner being. In the channel of the spaces we pass through, we extend and transform ourselves; the narrator in us speaks and sees in different ways, imagines in other modes. New frontiers, new shapes of the possible, open up within.

The journey in the photograph is the closest thing to a poem: both are exercises in perceiving the unknown, attempts to inhabit new worlds, even if only with the eyes. The camera registers the essential experience: the appearance of the poetic image, the original moment that is the source of consciousness. The image that crystallizes is a medium of knowledge, a halting language struggling to be born.

Skin gives us a body, with volume and size. The body of our consciousness, though, is other: it conforms to the space of our vision. The gaze is formed by many frontiers, now the wall facing us, now the distant horizon; it flows through the spaces we look at as through a channel or conduit, including whatever it touches in the mass of the visible. The body of consciousness changes shape constantly as it travels. Within it we enlarge ourselves and lose ourselves, pass from distraction to amazement, from the old and familiar to the unknown. The poetic image is like a handhold, or a root, locating us in the vast and passive space that is the eye's domain.

*(continued on page 60)*

Abbas, *Dust Storm*, Oapan, Guerrero, Mexico, 1987

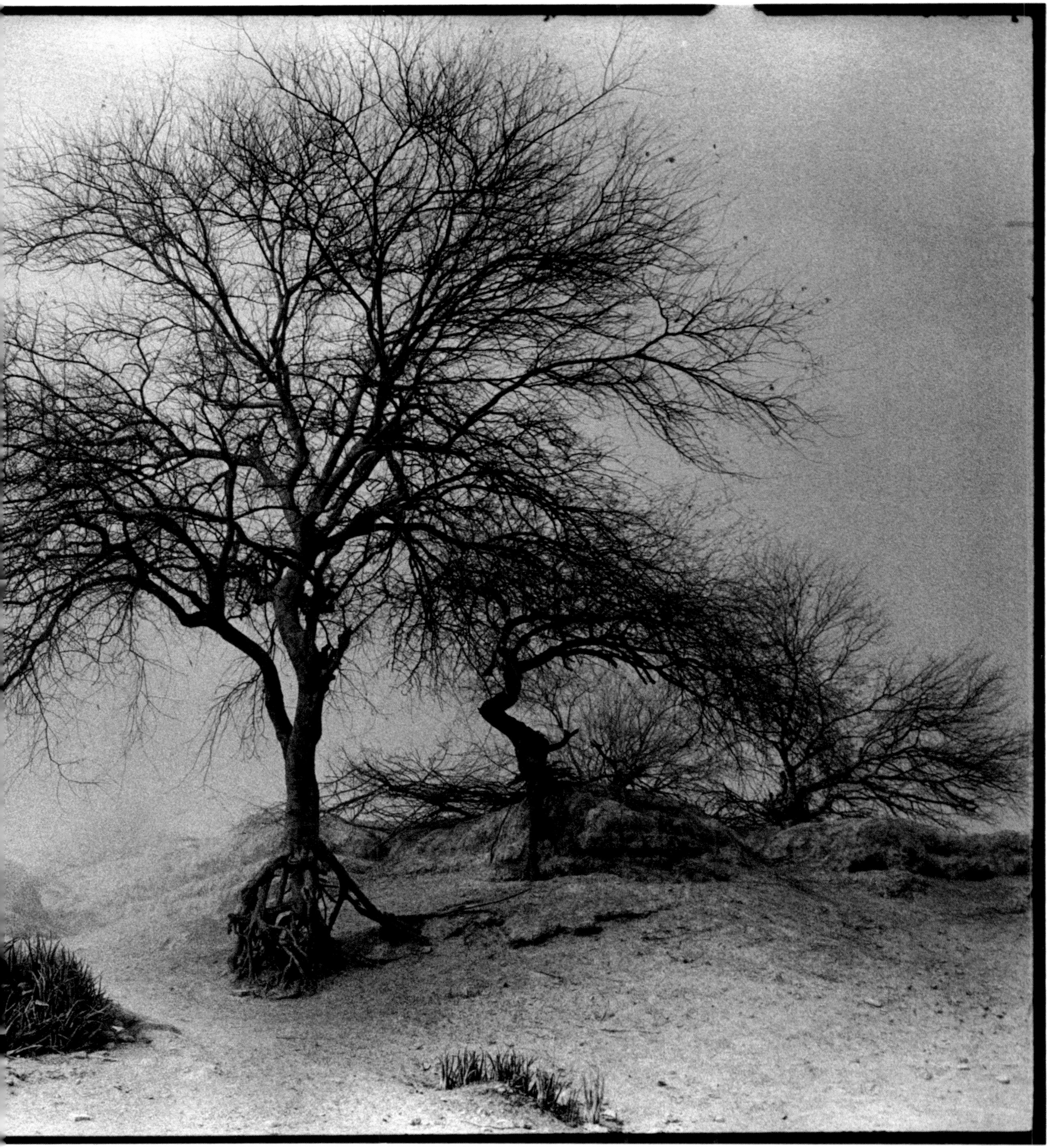

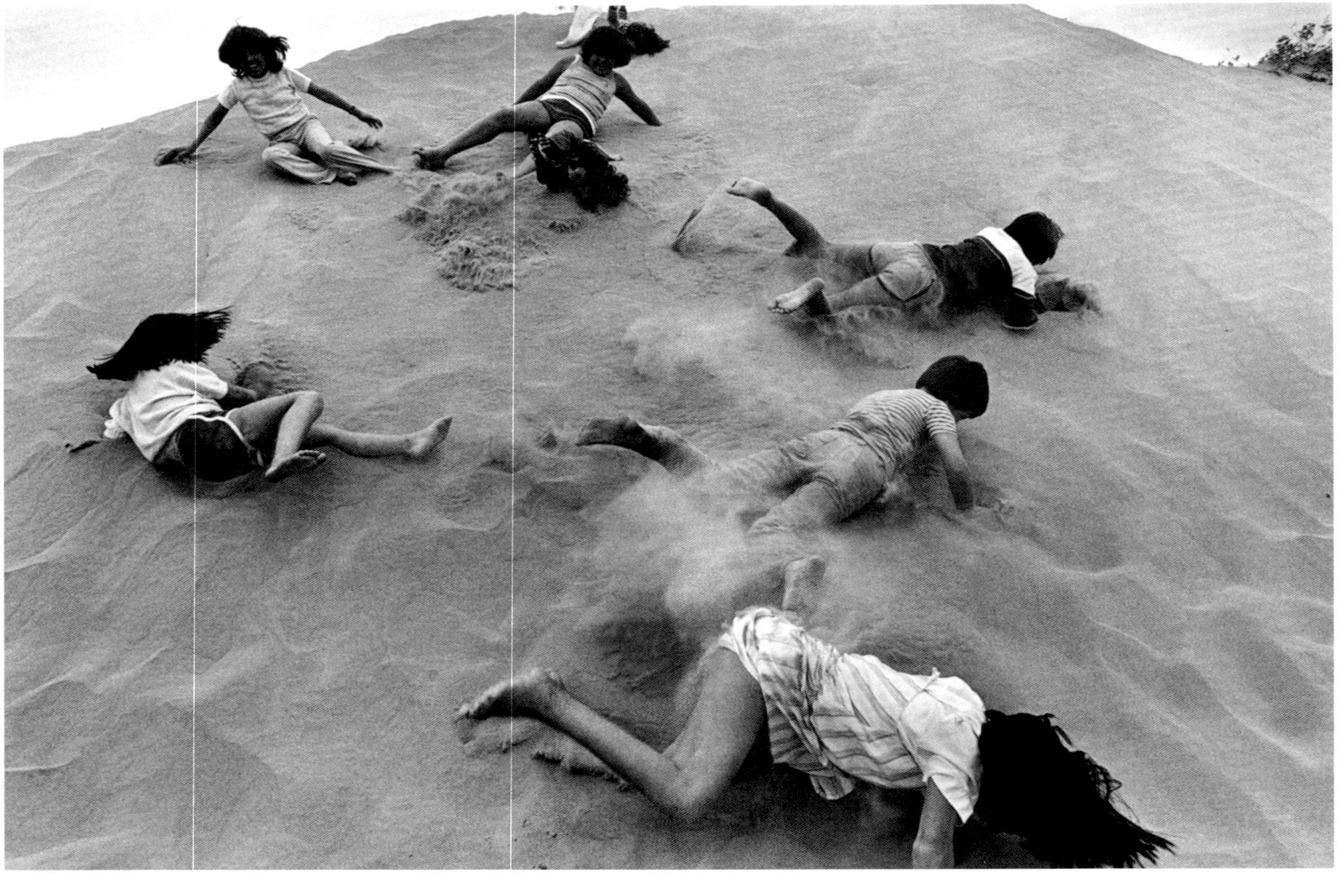

Graciela Iturbide, *Primer día del verano* (First day of summer), Veracruz, Mexico, 1982

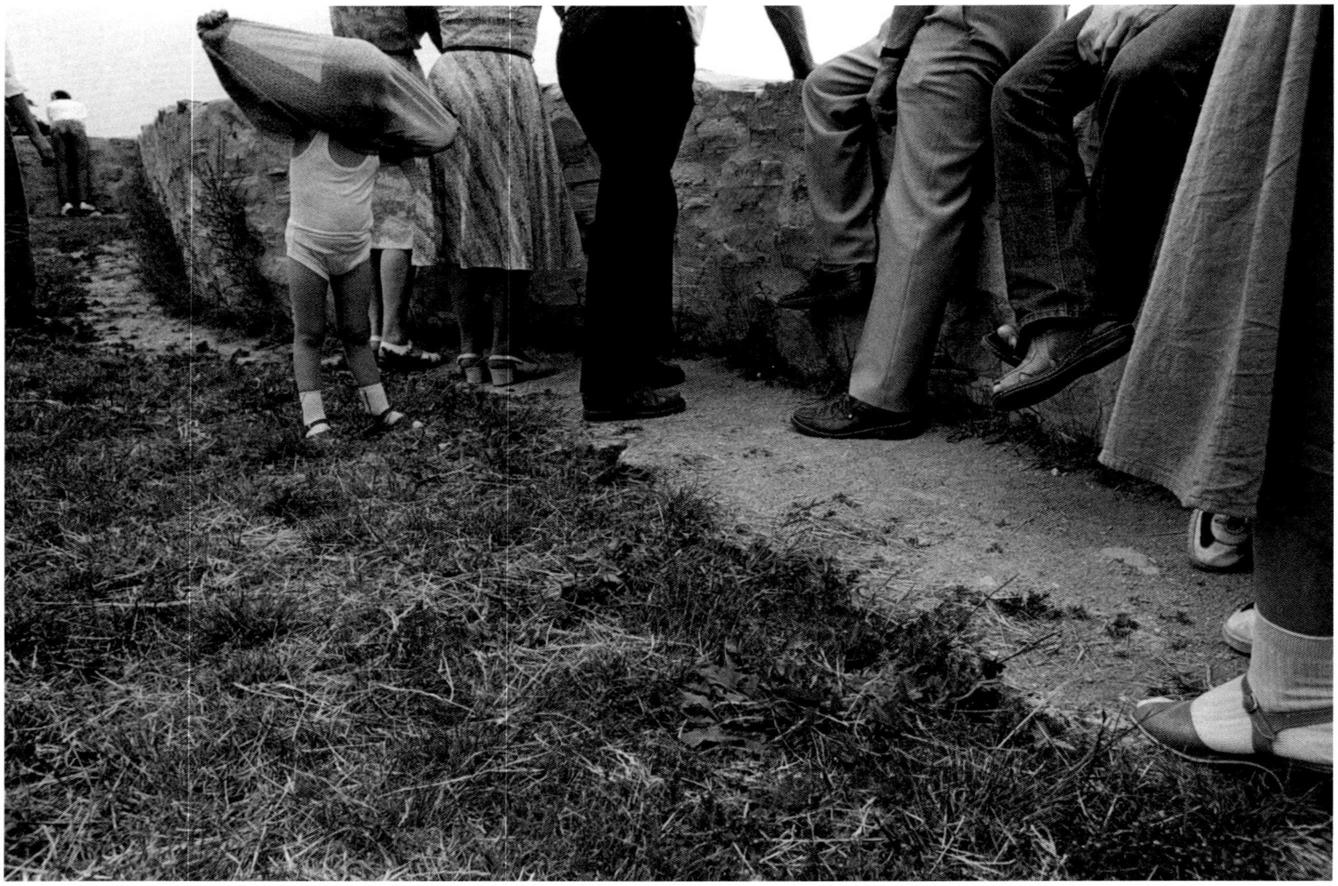

Graciela Iturbide, *El mundo de los mayores* (The world of the grown-ups), East Germany, 1981

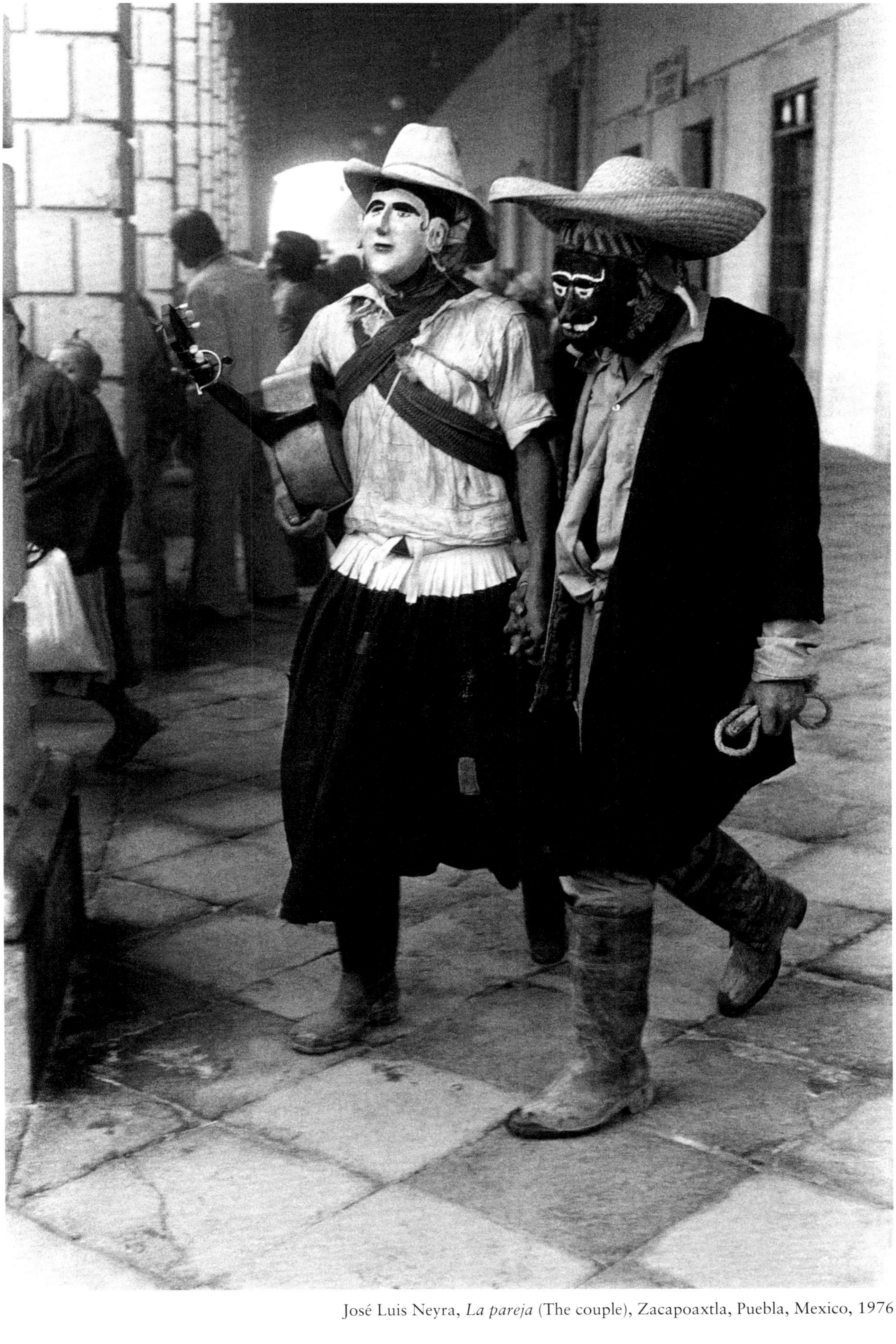

José Luis Neyra, *La pareja* (The couple), Zacapoaxtla, Puebla, Mexico, 1976

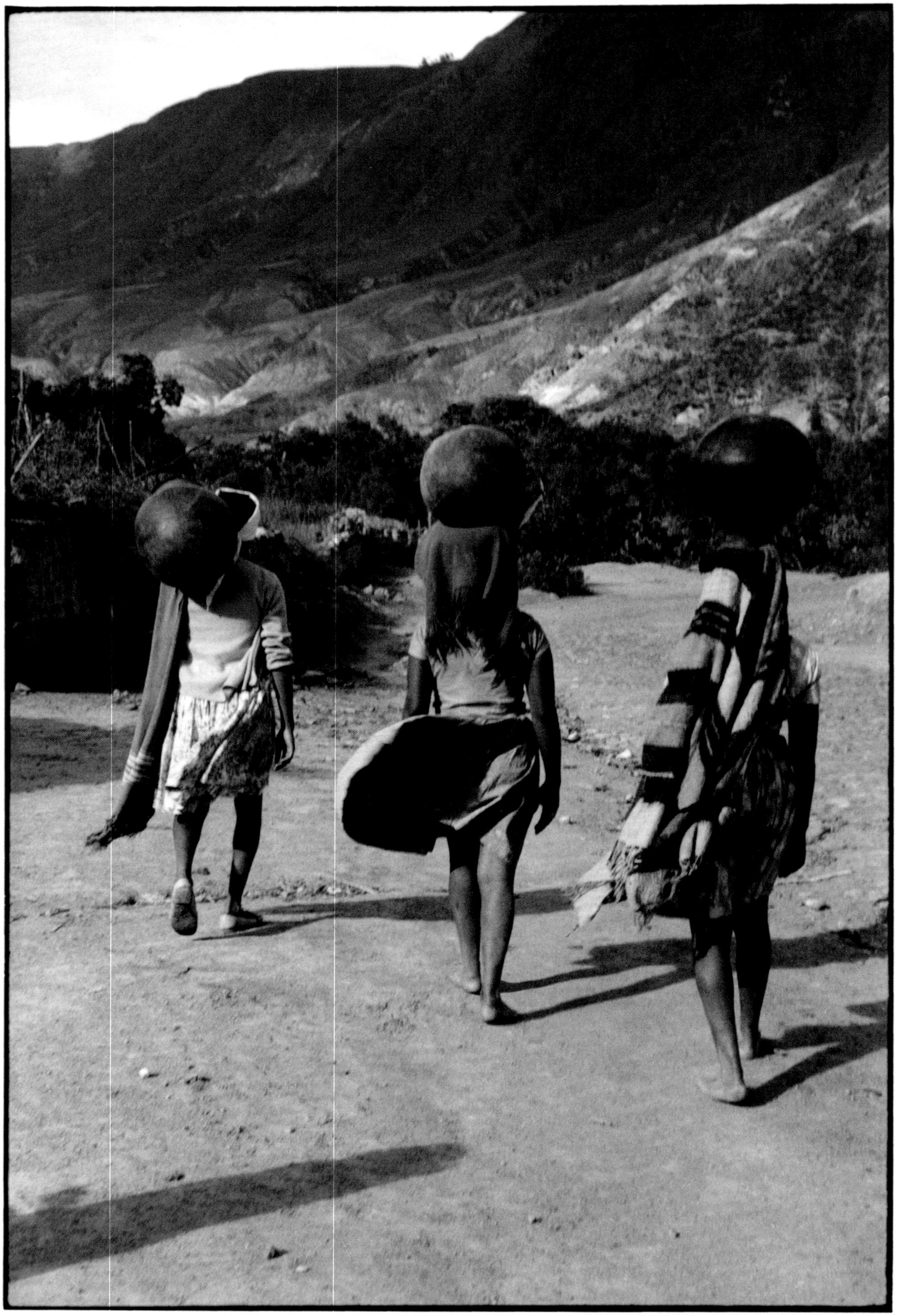

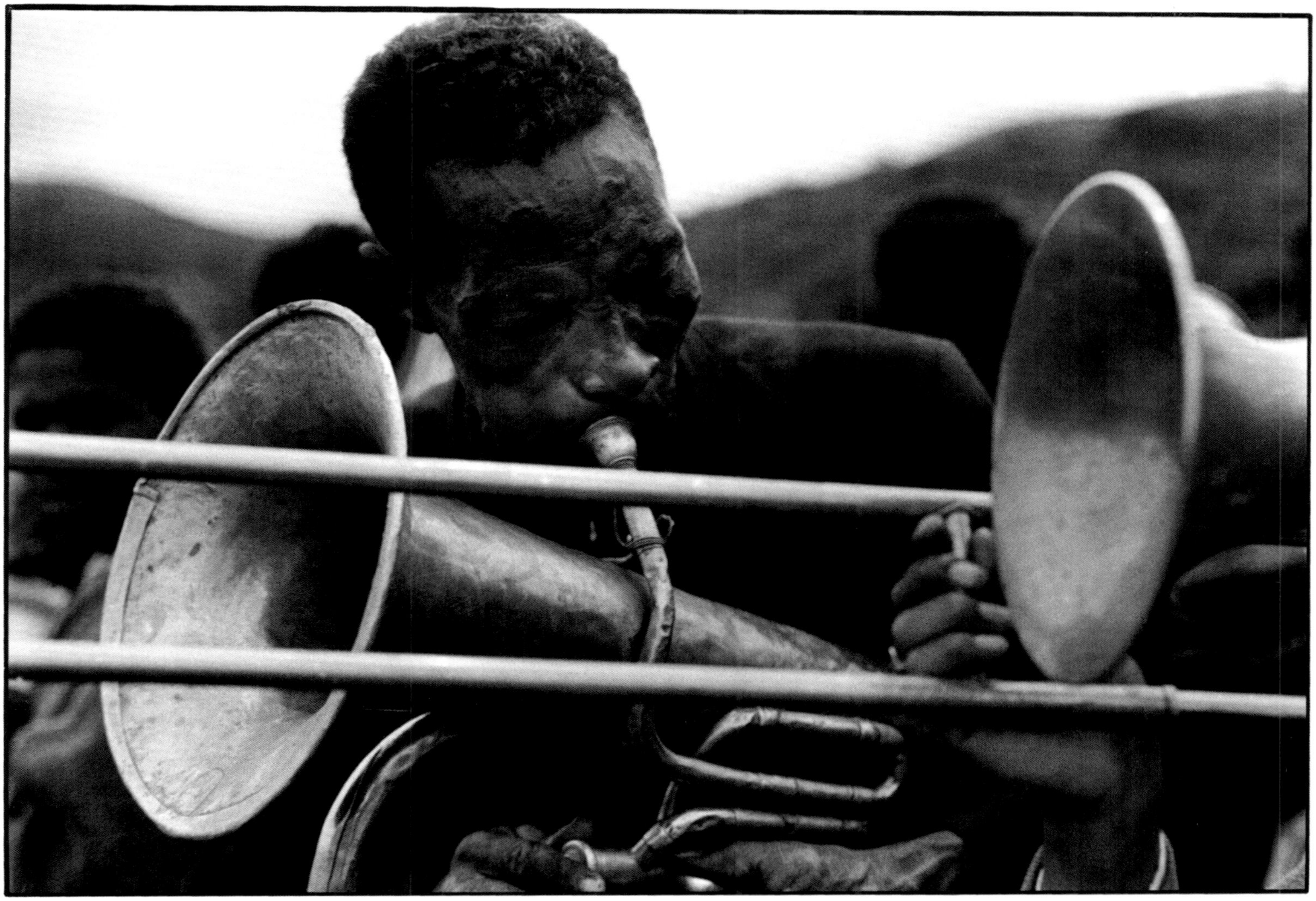

Hugo Cifuentes, *El músico mayor* (The greatest musician), Ecuador, 1980

*Opposite*: Hugo Cifuentes, *Las aguateras* (The water carriers), Ecuador, 1980

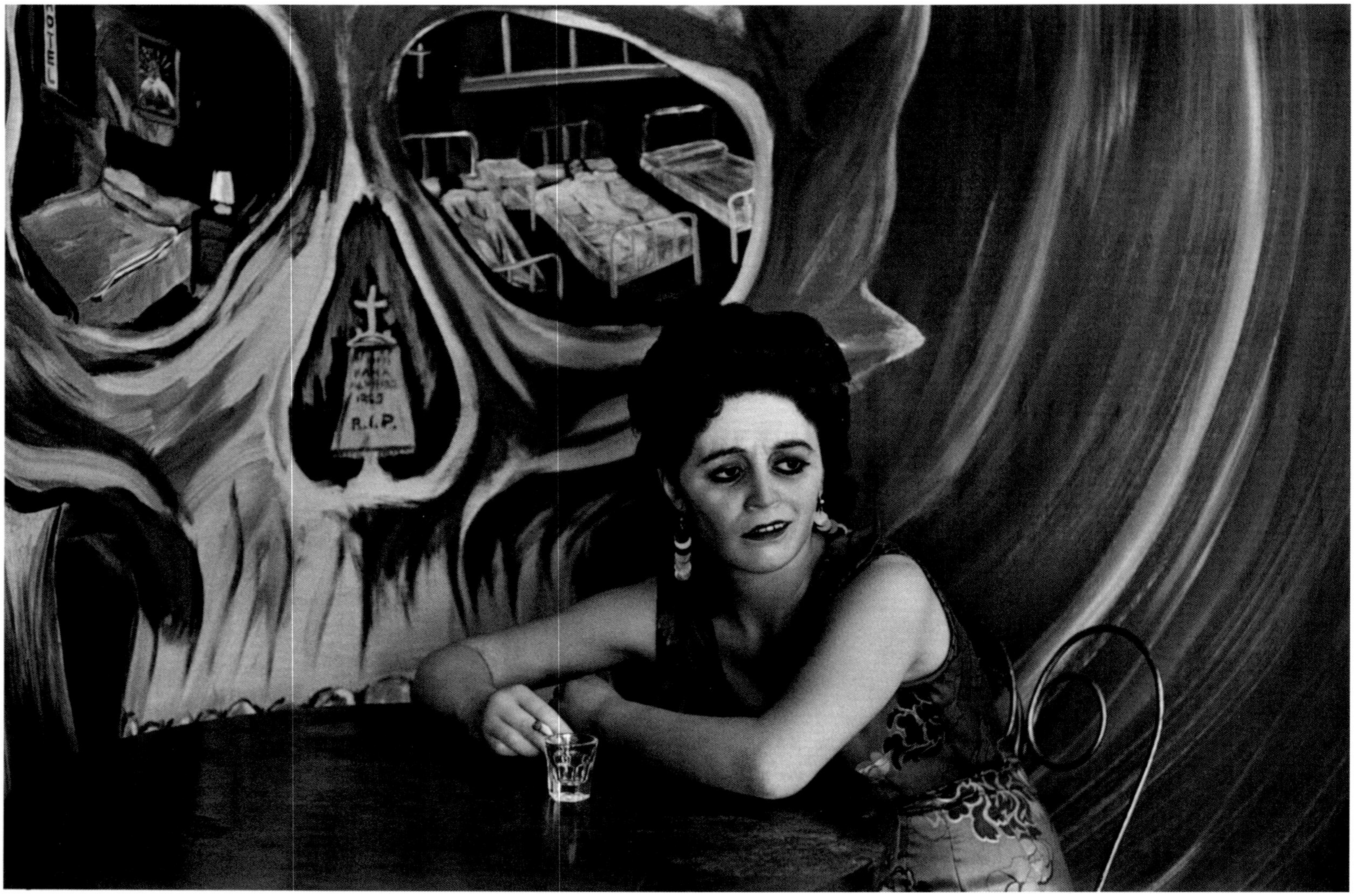


Graciela Iturbide, *El matrimonio* (The marriage), Panama, 1974

*Opposite*: Graciela Iturbide, *Inmaculada* (The Virgin Mary), Xochimilco, Mexico, 1984

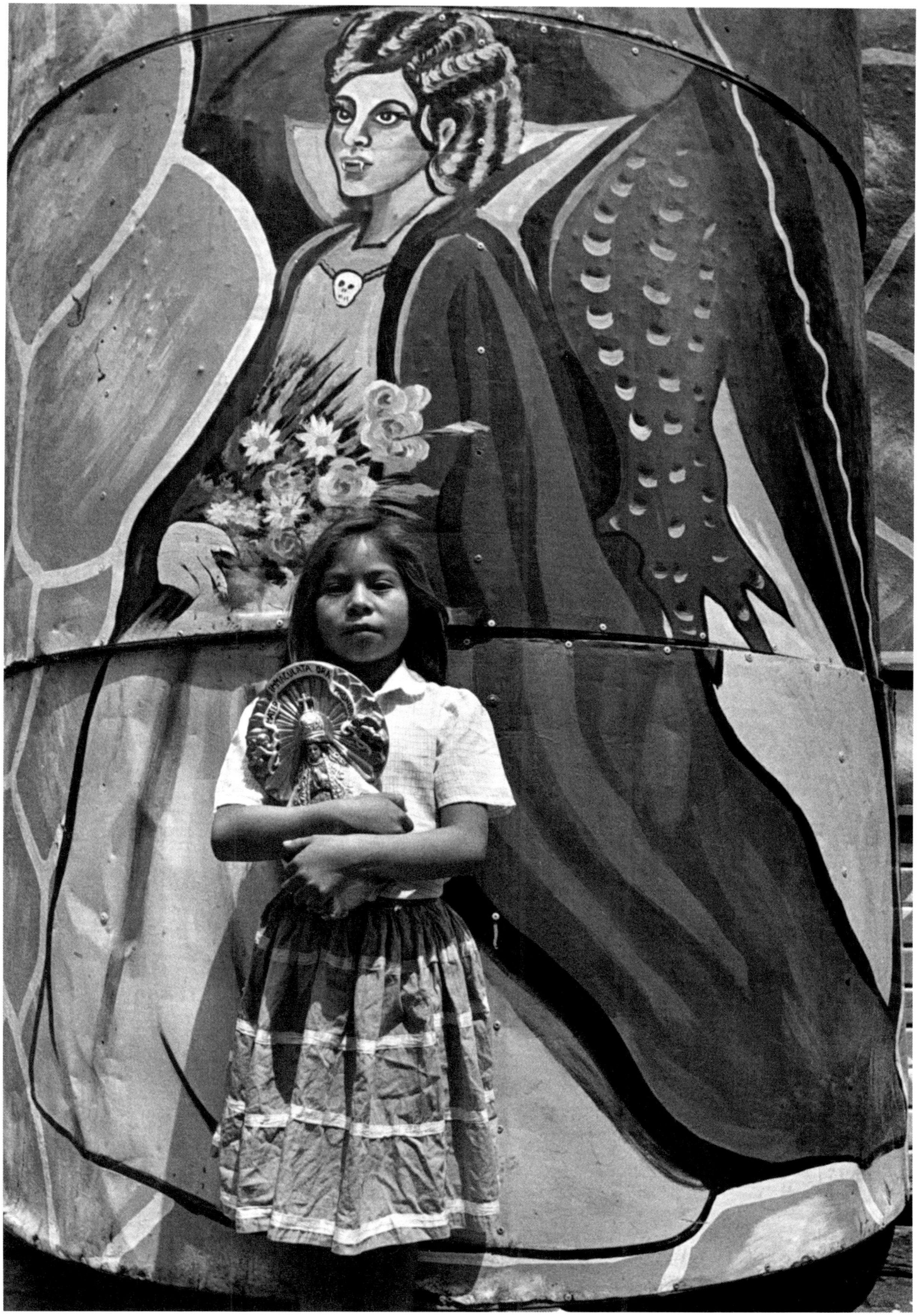

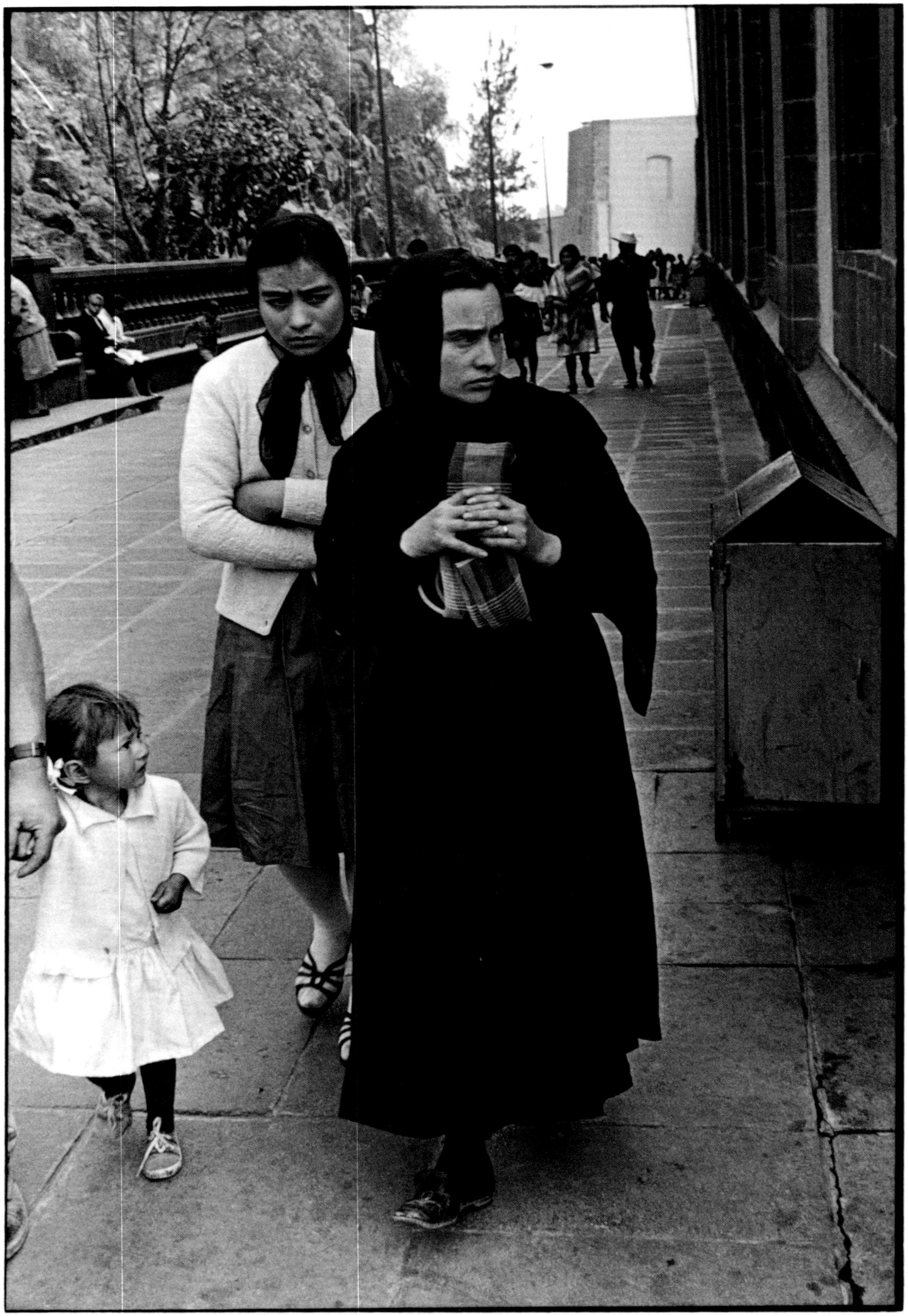

José Luis Neyra, *La monja* (The nun), La Villa de Guadalupe, Mexico City, Mexico, 1971

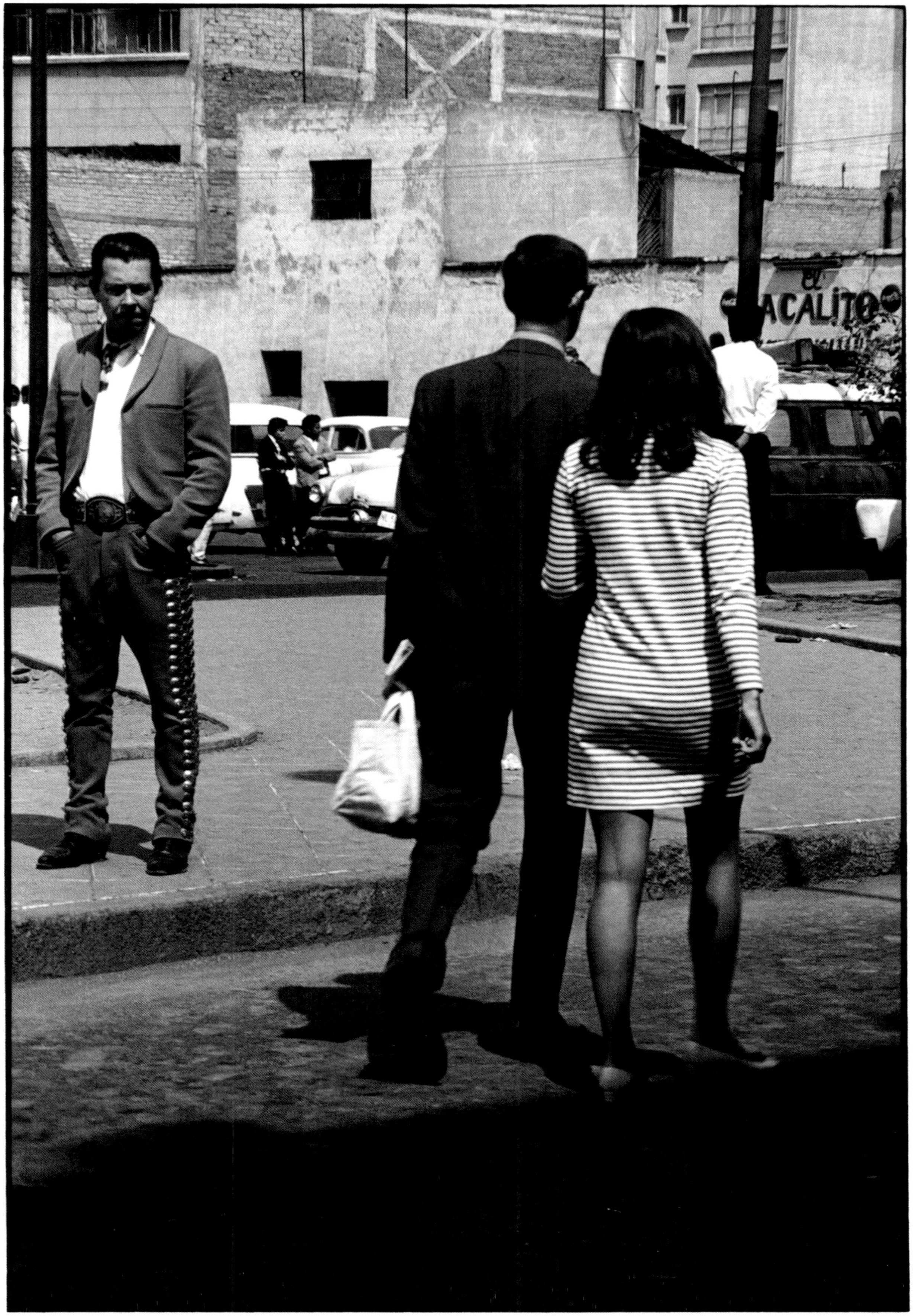

José Luis Neyra, *Plaza de Garibaldi*, Mexico City, Mexico, 1968

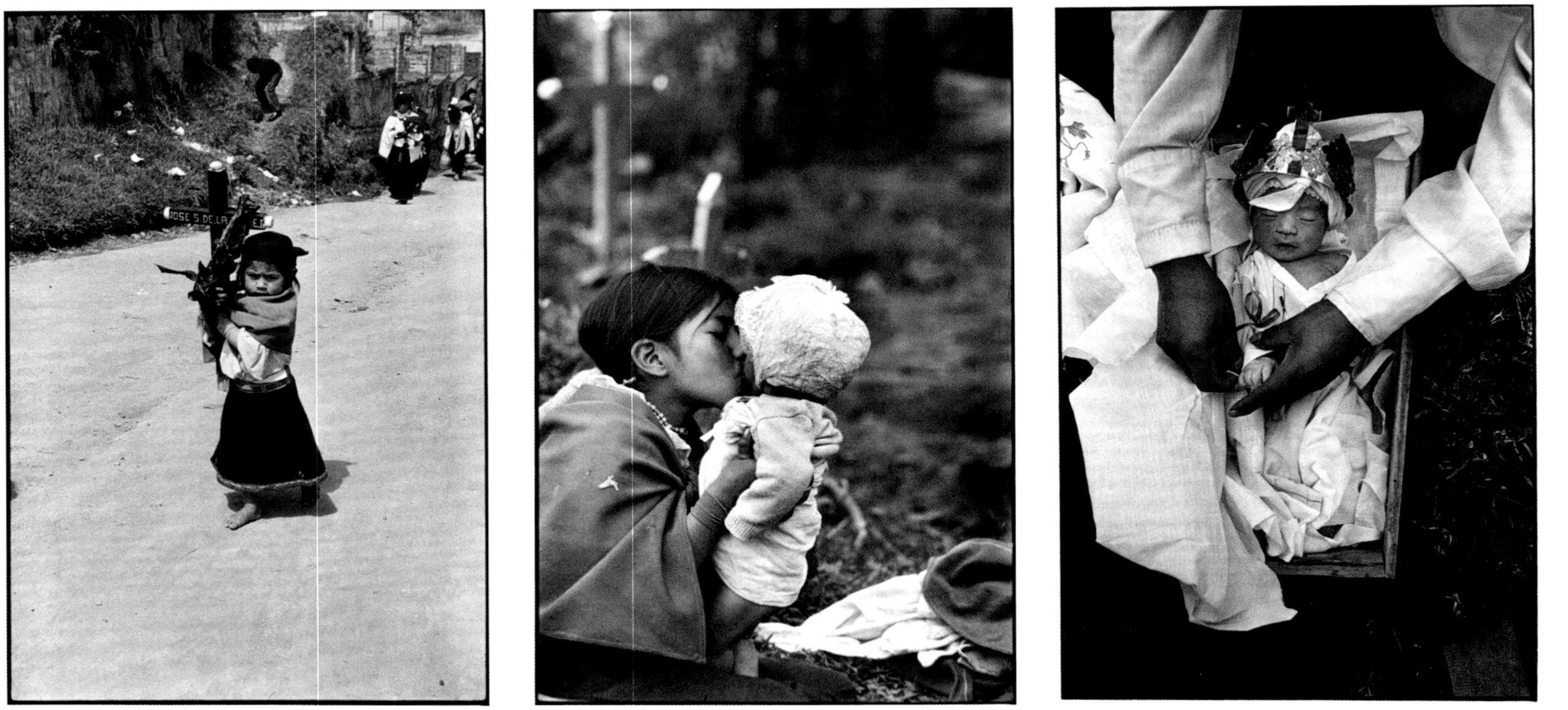

Hugo Cifuentes, from the series "Huañurca," Ecuador, 1982

There we perceive and receive ourselves, recover ourselves, grasp and understand ourselves. Abandoning the neutral surface of the given, the poetic image enters the depths of links and language. In the ocean imposed by the eye, it once again takes on skin, bone, muscles, strength—once again grants us substance.

Touched by poetry, the photograph acts like a mirror: the world is in it, but so are we. It captures and expresses us. We may be looking at external referents—the image of a mountain, a tree, the face of a child—but these images allow themselves to be inhabited by us, as the figure in a dream is inhabited by the dreamer. In the oneiric universe, every character and object represents, or is performed by, the one who dreams. The dreamer *is* what is dreamed—dust, tree, stone. That is why the term *obra de autor* (author's work) is used for the kind of photograph that aims to discover the poetic image. Every poetic image becomes our own, becomes our soul, is in some way dreamed, the receptacle of our reveries.

Gaston Bachelard, in his *Poetics of Space* (1969), argues that every poetic image has a degree of reverberation and a degree of resonance. Reverberation is rapture, ecstasy, and influences the soul; resonance is heard in the space of the spirit, in the whole mesh of echoes and connotations that the image awakens. In its quality of resonance the image speaks in the third person, displaying the orchestration of its networks; in its quality of reverberation, on the other hand, the image speaks in the first person, engaging us in a dialogue, taking possession of us. Our soul inhabits the poetic image and is made manifest through it.

In confronting one of Abbas's photographs, then, something in us is transformed into that striated grove, damaged by dust storms, the trees like nerves numbed by the cold of the open country. Reverberation reveals the self, capturing it in the splinter of the image, that fragment of a whole, of a lost language. The image returns body to us from the soul; it forms us, communes with us.

In one of Graciela Iturbide's photographs, children roll in sand, jubilant planets hurled down a steep slope toward an abyss. We share in the image's giddiness and charm. A yearning is fulfilled in every poetic encounter: subject and object are united, mingled. They join in an intimacy. But this is also an archetypal game, and in the photograph the linear time of reality encounters the archetype of myth, the landmark of desire, the meaning of dream. A poetic image fabricates us, gives substance to a shadow.

One never knows when the miracle will occur—when the eyes of alien beings meet, as in Neyra's work; in the bric-a-brac of Flores Olea's back rooms; or in Cifuentes's doll-like dead baby. The poetic image appears not only as body or presence, but as sign, as promise of meaning, as glyph to disentangle. It implicates us in its enigma, captures us in its wonder, makes us inhabit it.

The moment when external perception and an unknown impulse come together: that is the poetic image. Something of ourselves always comes to life in the presence of the unknown, the other, the strange. In the poetic image, we wish to be in some way born to ourselves.

Translated from the Spanish by Cola Franzen

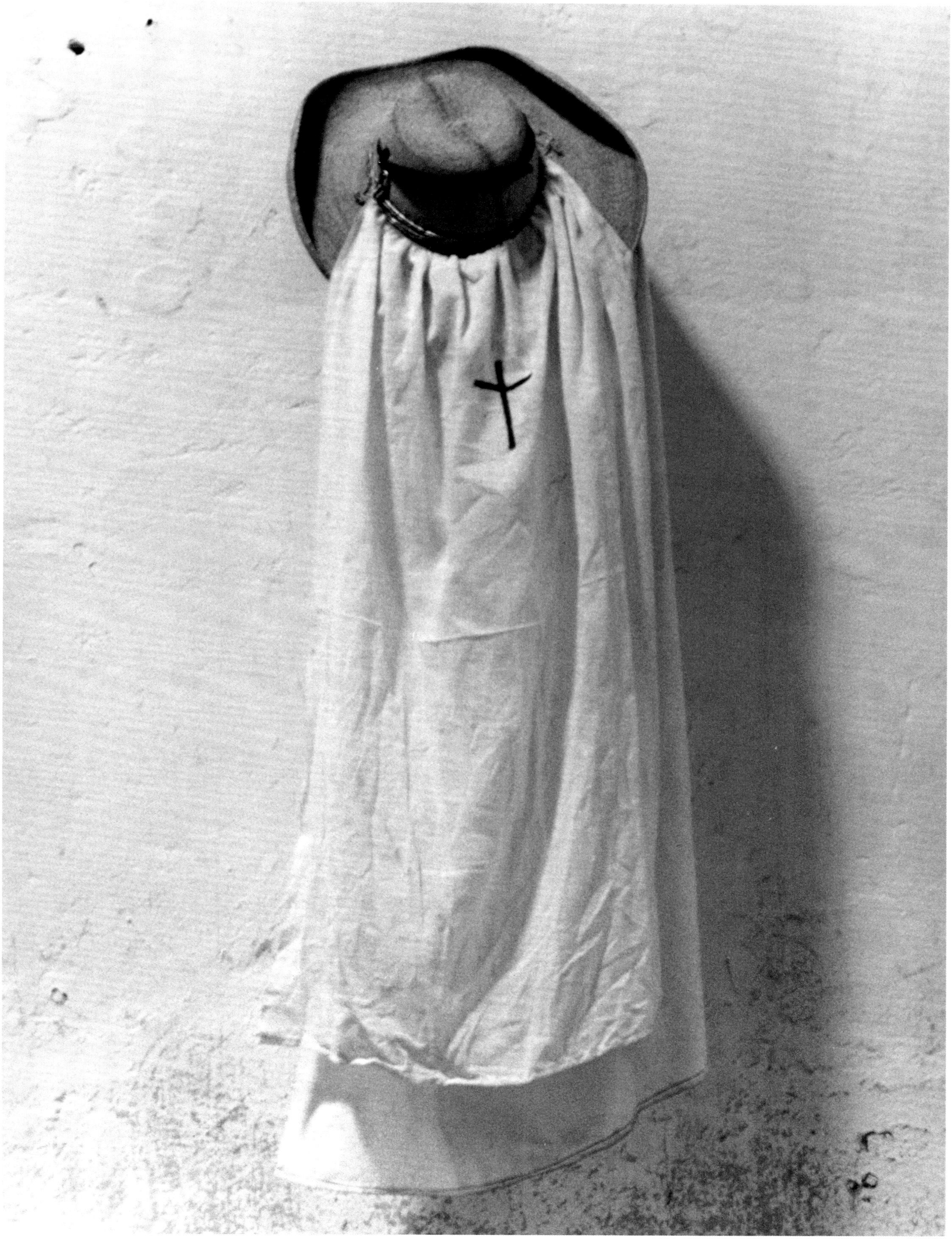

Rafael Doniz, untitled, Atotonilco, Guanajuato, Mexico, 1985

# Natural History of Things

Some objects never travel. So they endure, immune to oblivion and the most strenuous labors imposed by use and time; arrested in an eternity of parallel instants that interweave nothingness and habit. Such a singular condition posits them at the fringes of life's tide and fever. There, they remain untroubled by doubt or terror, and the burgeoning that keeps watch is but a faint trace of their pointless duration.

—Álvaro Mutis, *Caravansary*

Hay objetos que no viajan nunca. Permanecen así, inmunes al olvido y a las más arduas labores que imponen el uso y el tiempo. Se detienen en una eternidad hecha de instantes paralelos que entretejen la nada y la costumbre. Esa condición singular los coloca al margen de la marea y la fiebre de la vida. No los visita la duda ni el espanto y la vegetación que los vigila es apenas una tenue huella de su vana duración. —Álvaro Mutis, *Caravansary*

## HISTORIA NATURAL DE LAS COSAS

**By Álvaro Mutis**

By day: things sleep. By night: they dissolve—
and often never return. Then there are
those who've come by this unlawful
privilege of revealing wood, walls, objects
signs, rubble, windows, and stones.
These frenzied personae
invented the litany of images
to be regarded, in short, by the reader.
I don't envy them. They know too much.
For things are not the trace nor are they
the symbol of human passage. Things
can barely claim from us that first impulse,
that initial feint charge that leads them
to the inviolate labyrinth of representation.
They begin to fend, things do, for themselves,
they begin to shed the inner vestige
that named us, finally settled
in their own existence, the lustral
waters in which they are preserved.
What, if not our habitual clumsiness,
can presume that things have weight
and are subject to the immutable physics
that affirms their folly? No. This is hardly
news to us. Things follow a different course
and, at a crossroads known only to them,
they're met by these gold miners of nothingness:
photographers of a time that doesn't transpire.
It's nobody's business but theirs. From now on,
I absolve myself of their enterprise. They ventured
afar in their travels. Long ago, things took leave
of us to settle other reaches, and to manifest
a peculiar form of survival there.
They've turned their backs on us and, now,
we're the only debris that's left,
voiceless objects with no destiny.
It's useless to exhaust ourselves in the struggle
to provide things with a place
they have no place in.

Las cosas duermen de día. De noche
se disuelven y, a menudo, jamás regresan.
Hay seres que detentan el privilegio
de revelarnos maderas, objetos, muros,
signos, escombros, cristales, piedras.
Esos alucinados personajes
inventaron la letanía de imágenes
que el lector verá en seguida.
No los envidio. Saben demasiado.
Porque las cosas no son huella
ni símbolo del paso del hombre.
De él las cosas reciben, apenas,
ese primer impulso, esa inicial
y tenue energía que las conduce
al intacto laberinto de las representaciones.
Y van viviendo, las cosas, por su cuenta,
van perdiendo el rastro
que en ellas nos nombraba
y acaban instaladas en su propia existencia,
en el agua lustral que las mantiene.
¿Qué, sino nuestra sólita torpeza,
puede pretender que las cosas
tengan peso y estén sujetas
a la física inmutable
que insiste en su propia necedad?
No. Ya lo sabemos. Las cosas toman otro camino
y en una encrucijada, sólo por ellos conocida,
las esperan estos gambusinos de la nada:
los fotógrafos de un tiempo que no fluye.
Allá ellos. Desde ahora me desligo
de su empresa. Muy lejos se atrevieron
en su viaje. Hace mucho que las cosas
nos dejaron para poblar otros dominios
y manifestar allí su especial supervivencia.
Nos han dado la espalda y, ahora,
somos nosotros los únicos escombros,
objetos sin voz y sin destino.
Inútil desgastarnos en la brega
de otorgar a las cosas un sitio
que no les pertenece.

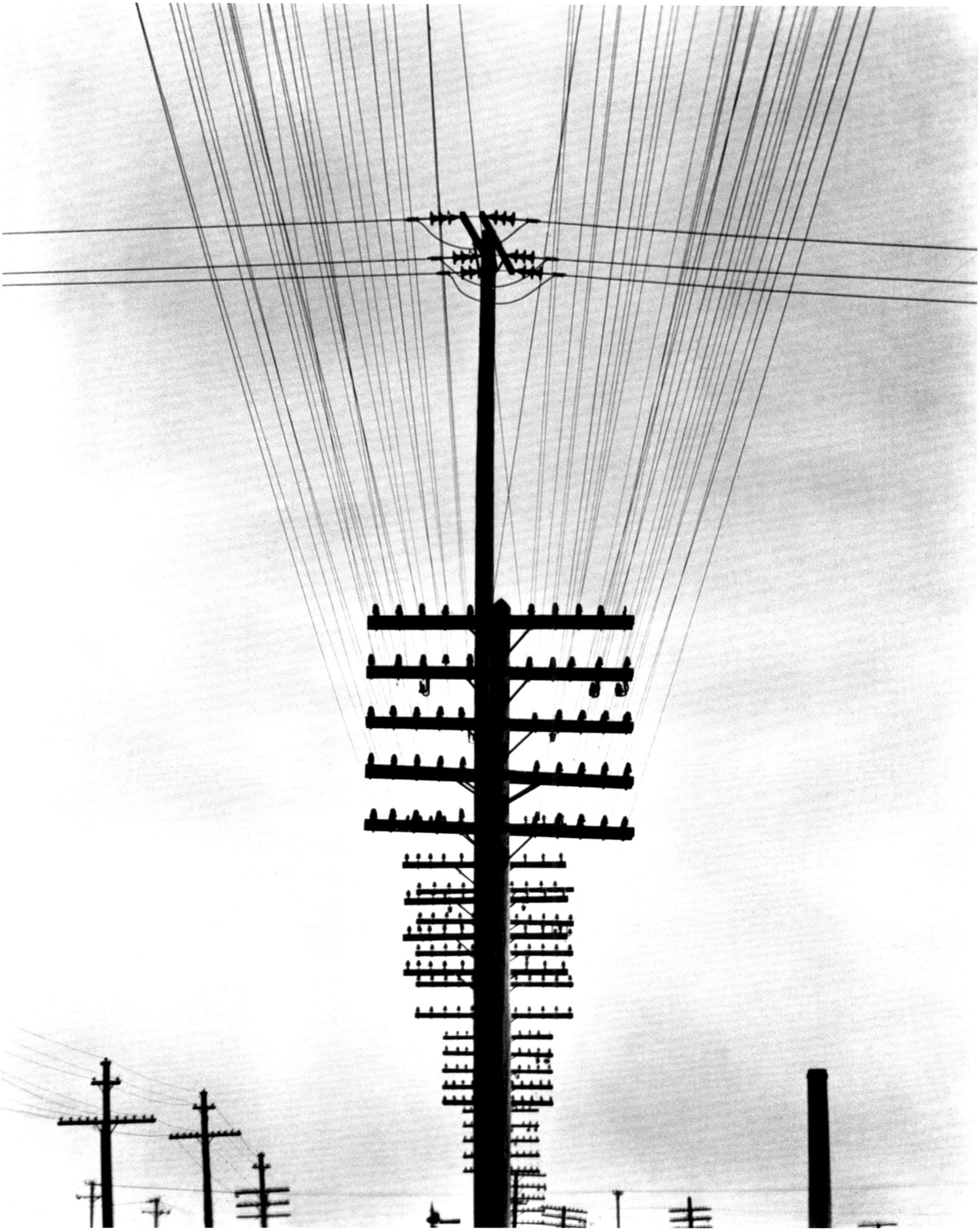

Tina Modotti, *Postes* (Poles), Mexico, ca. 1926

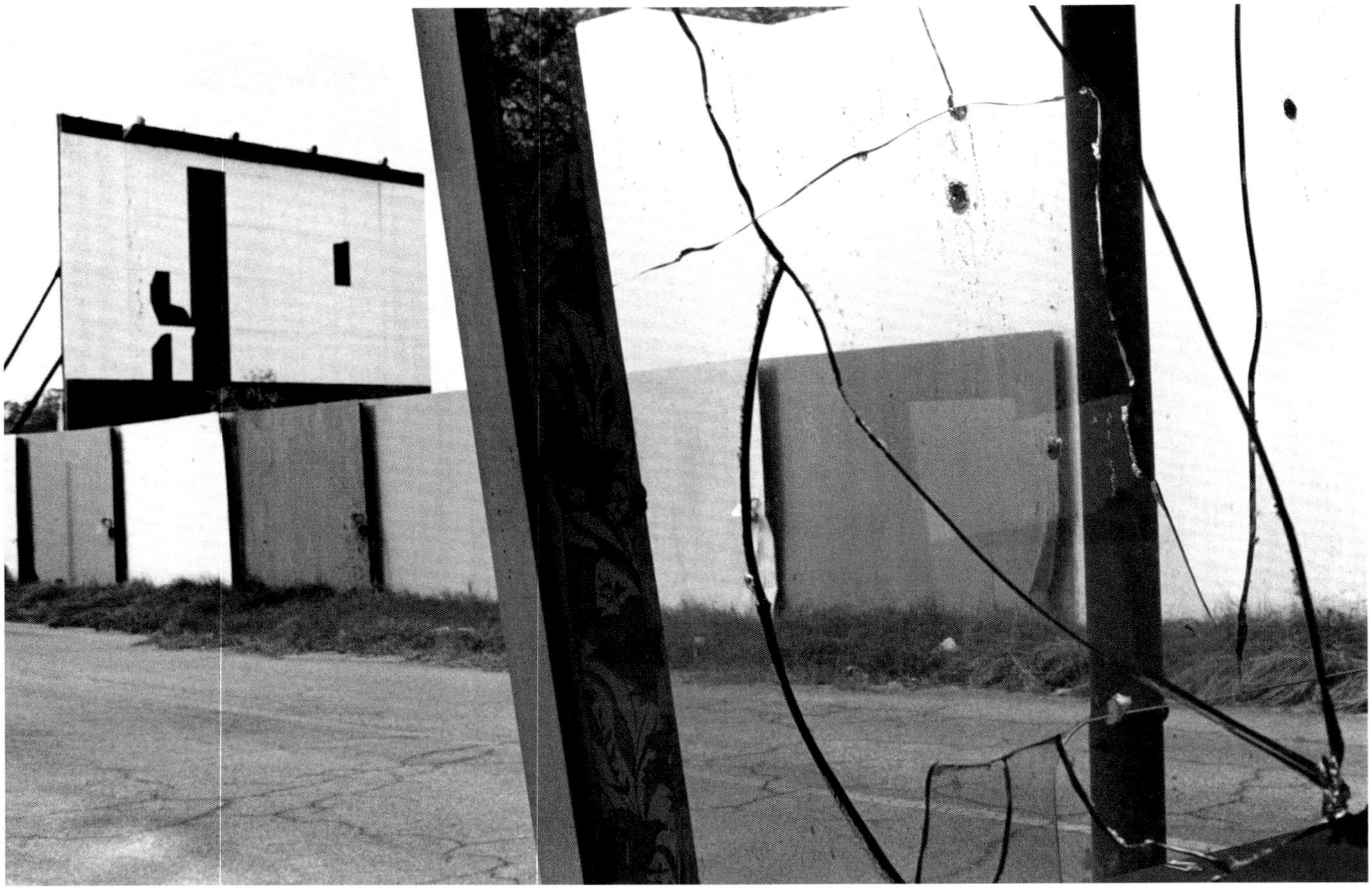

Laura Cohen, from the series "Balnearios" (Seaside resorts), France, 1984

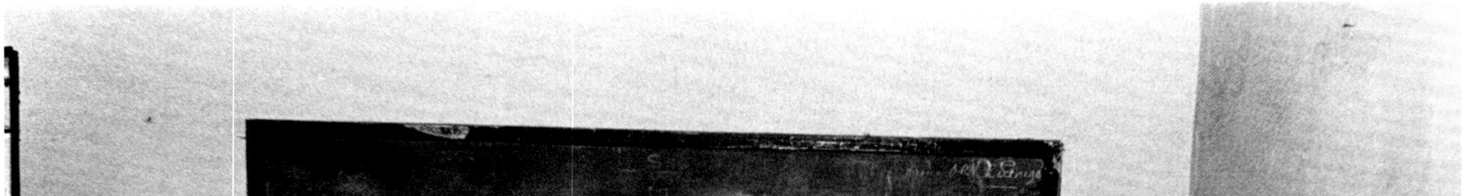

Agustín Martínez Castro, *Al maestro con cariño* (To the teacher with love), Mexico City, Mexico, 1980

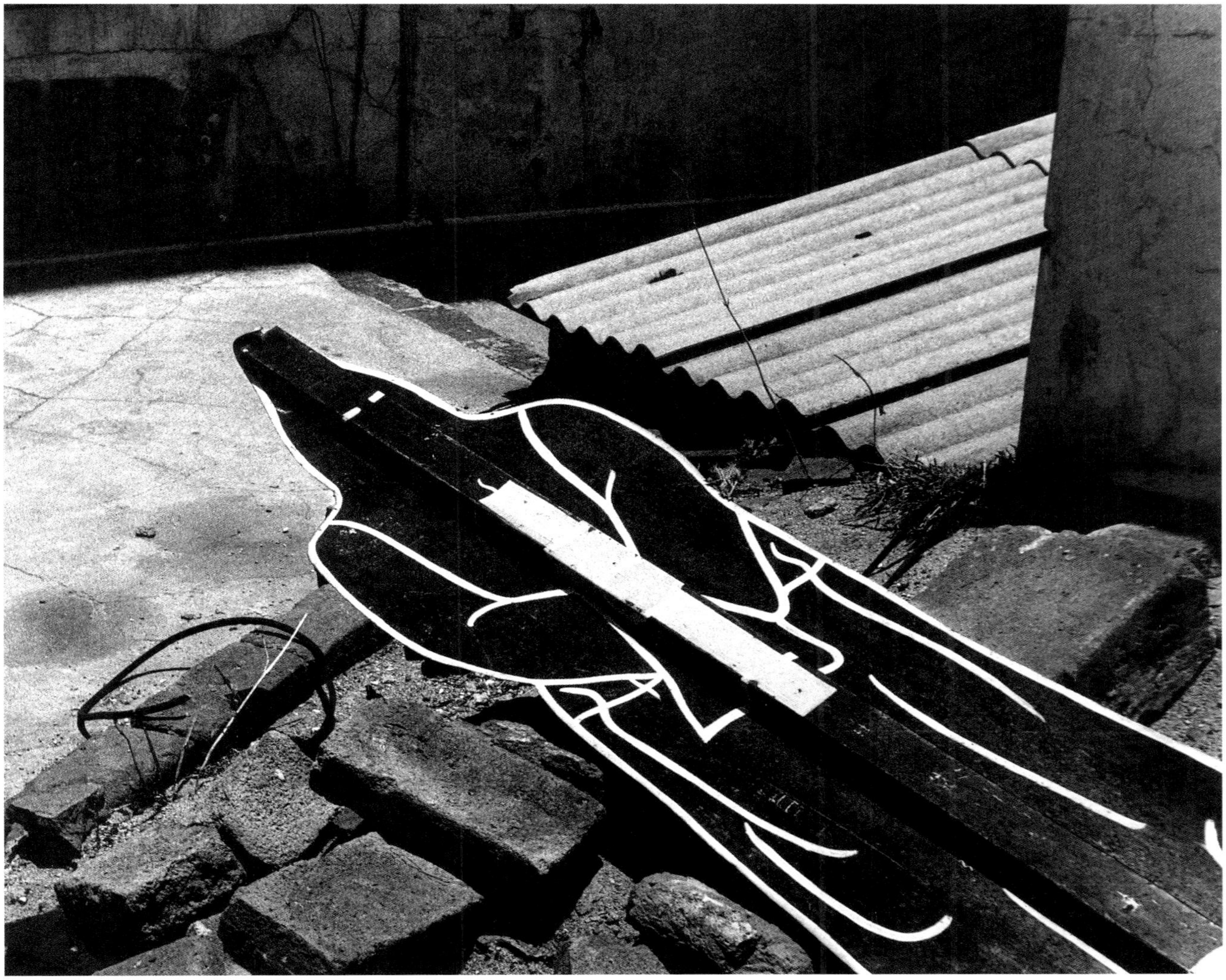

Elías Jaber, untitled, Guerrero, Mexico, 1980

Reader: drill your memory
and peruse these images. They're no longer
within your reach, will never return to you,
and never hold a secret for you again.
It's you now who reverts to nothing.
Wooden benches at the end of a mine.
A spotted jacket and vest.
Mannequins in their astonished nakedness.
The innocent mutation of litter.
Cables against the sky.
Beds and fish.
Meticulous hats.
Plaster swine and harsh cactuses
against a storm. A rocket,
and the robes of a habit, ankle-length.
The stale eroticism of a bathing beauty
figurine with no one to own her.
Wineskins in the sun.
A codfish that forgot the seaman
on the bottle of Scott's Emulsion.

Lector: adiestra tu memoria,
recorre estas imágenes. No son ya
de tu dominio, no volverán a ti jamás,
ni guardan para ti secreto alguno.
Eres tú quien regresa hacia la nada.
Los bancos de madera en el fondo de la mina.
La casaca y el chaleco mancillados.
Los maniquíes en su atónito desnudo.
La inocente mutación de la basura.
Los cables contra el cielo.
Las camas y los peces.
Los sombreros minuciosos.
Los cerdos de yeso y los amargos cactus
con fondo de tormenta.
El cohete y los hábitos talares.
El manido erotismo de la bañista
que nunca tendrá dueño.
Los odres al sol.
El bacalao que olvidó el marino
de la Emulsión de Scott.

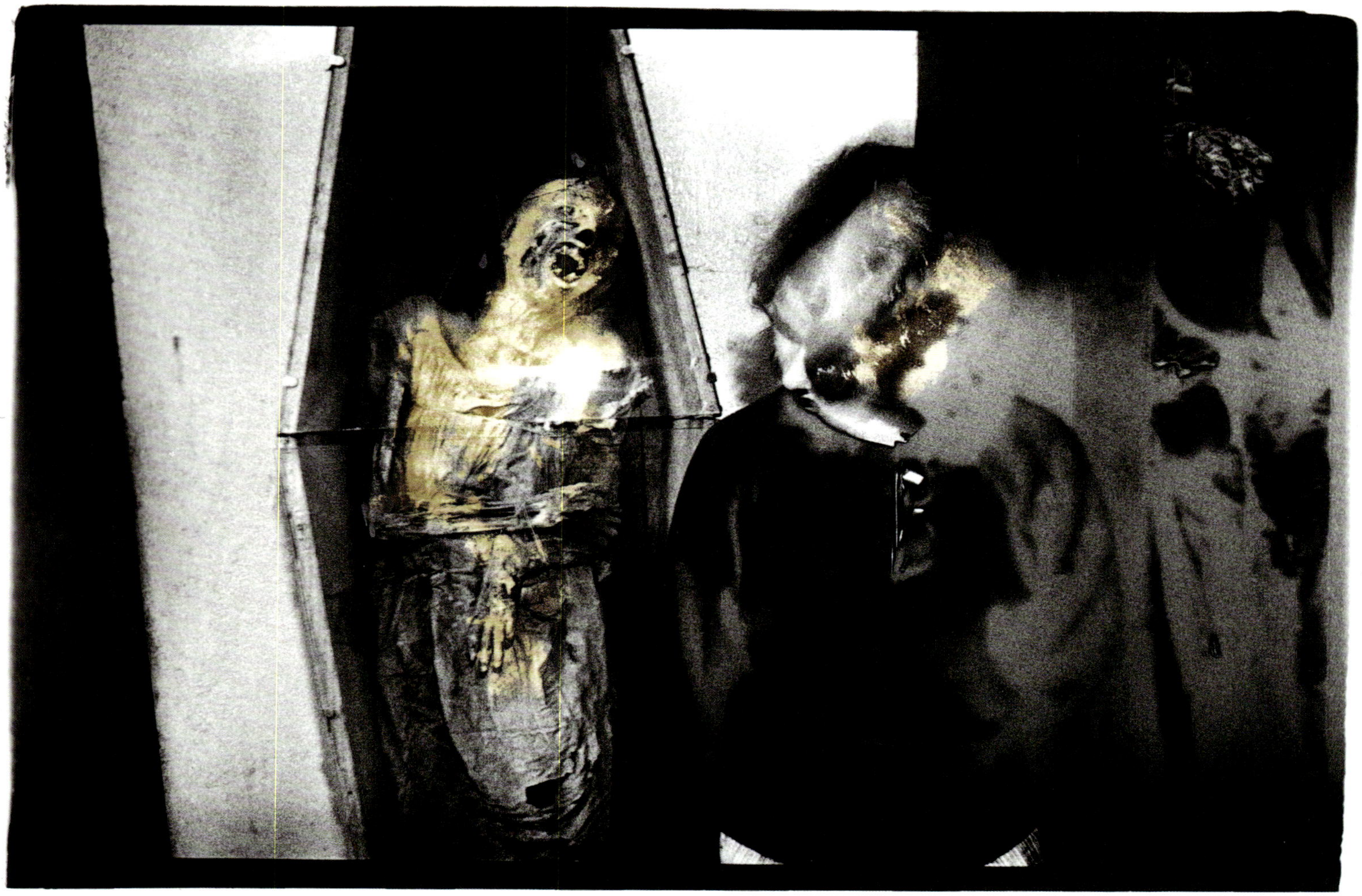

Rubén Ortiz Torres, *Retrato de vida y muerte* (Portrait of life and death), Guanajuato, Mexico, 1983

Vague forgotten gardens.
A gloomy episode of ice.
The song on that corner in colors more steadfast
and in plainer view than life itself.
Wood, and its essential knots.
That figure of Christ, fleeing torture.
The unsounded stupidity of a wax figure.
Walls, and more walls,
faces peering from what-never-happened,
canvas of a weathered wall, its
collapse inconceivable.
And the wind passing or the air motionless
and so many other things I'm going to name
as they elude language and, nonetheless,
are there, sleepless in the night,
watched over by minute constellations.
Behold. They're all in their order. Take
a good look: maybe now we can steal
an instant from death—just waiting to be let in.

Translated from the Spanish by Roberto Tejada

Los vagos jardines olvidados.
El hielo y su fúnebre episodio.
La canción de esa esquina con colores
más tercos y evidentes que la vida.
La madera y sus nudos esenciales.
Ese Cristo que huye del suplicio.
La estulticia insondable de las figuras de cera.
Los muros, otra vez los muros,
rostros de lo que nunca ha sucedido,
lienzos de lastimada pared cuyo derrumbe
se antoja inconcebible.
Y el viento que pasa o el aire detenido
y tantas otras cosas que voy a nombrar
y evaden la palabra y, sin embargo,
allí están, despiertas en la noche,
vigiladas por minúsculas constelaciones.
Allí están. Todas en su orden allí están.
Mírenlas bien: tal vez así ganemos un instante
a la muerte que espera para entrar.

Pablo Ortiz Monasterio,
*Viernes Santo* (Good Friday),
Milpa Alta, Mexico, 1985

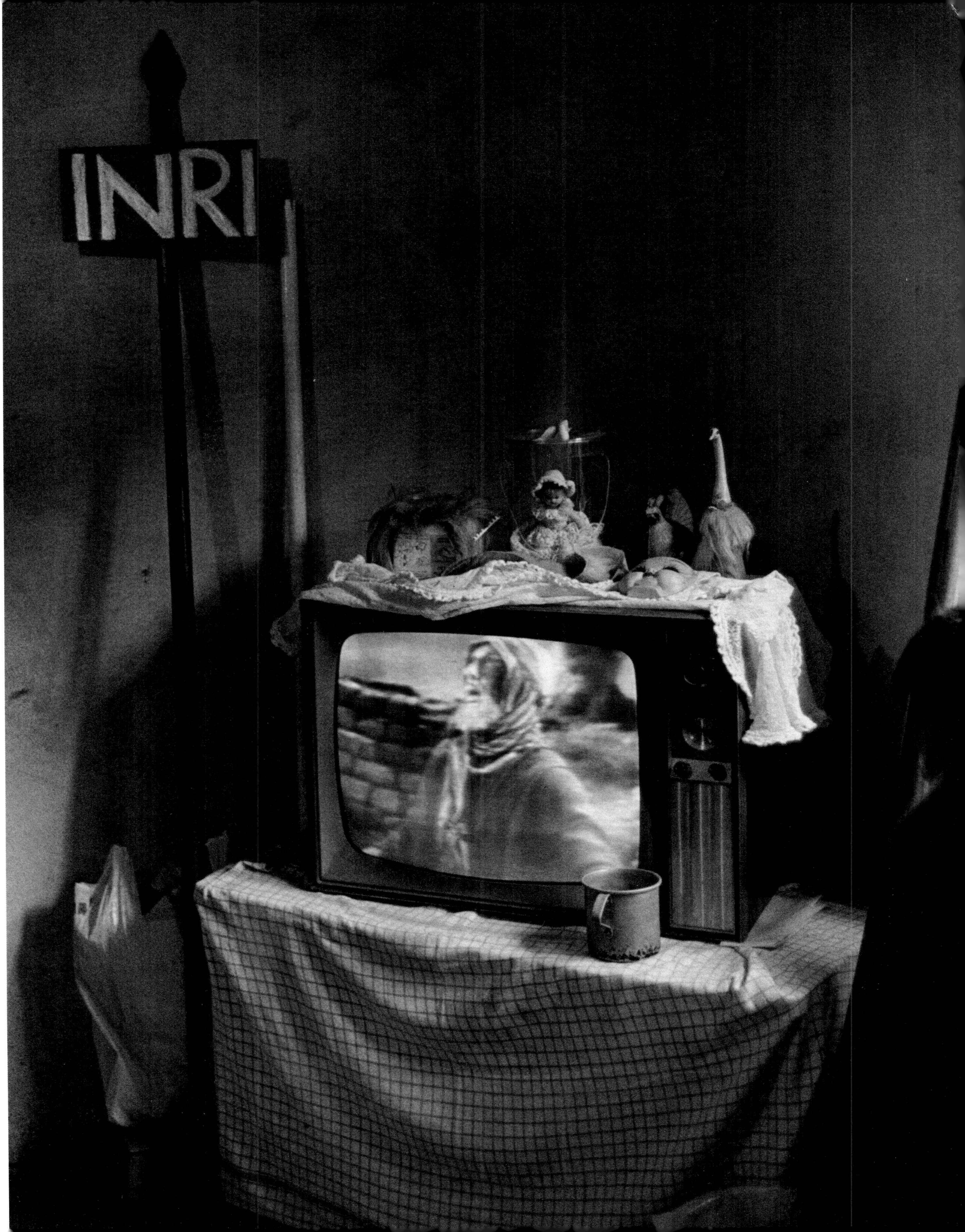
INRI

# Sweet Bitter Sweat

## MIGUEL RIO BRANCO

### By Roberto Tejada

Miguel Rio Branco's *Dulce sudor amargo* (Sweet bitter sweat), published as part of the Río de Luz series in 1985, brought together images taken around the seaport of Salvador, Bahia, Brazil's former colonial capital, where the photographer lived intermittently throughout the 1980s. An example of bold sequencing, the nearly eighty color photographs are a personal account of the complexity of contemporary Brazilian daily life—at least those aspects that manifest themselves in this cultural hub of the northeastern province of Bahia.

John Berger has written that the true content of a photograph is often invisible because it derives from "the intensity with which we are made aware of the poles of absence and presence." Both as individual statements and as narrative clusters, these images appeal first to the senses—the gold-orange folds of a curtain as flickered by the slant of a fading sun; the smell of sweet oils and saltpeter, of sweat and fortress stone; the crack of voices in the cadence of close quarters, or along the unshielded edges of the open sea, between men and women from windows and balconies, behind doors that blur into the street, or around a polychrome beach-front stand along Bahia de Todos os Santos. They manage to coax a vocal quality out of the color photograph, with restrained or sharp accents that raise moral and aesthetic questions about the medium itself.

In the work of Rio Branco, the senses become a legitimate means of inquiry, recognition, and knowledge. In one image, you can smell the listless sway of faded clothes hung out to dry. In another, you can hear an aimless dog slinking across a crumbled facade, or feel the confident strikes and the treacherous bearing of two men involved in *capoeira*. These isolated moments have specific cultural meanings. *Capoeira*'s syncretic form of self-defense and encoded violence, originated by African slaves, has endured a long history of repression and resistance that has survived to this day. A martial art often performed to percussive music, it is fused with elements that point to recreational sport, popular dance, and ritual observance.

In two other photographs, the dauntless and self-sufficient glare of a child peering from behind a weathered stone column offers a moment of respite from the view of a man shown facedown and apparently lifeless on the pavement, his ripped trousers exposing his buttocks and genitals—our eyes allowed to settle, instead, on the pink plastic bag over which he is sprawled. Drawing the view-

*(continued on page 74)*

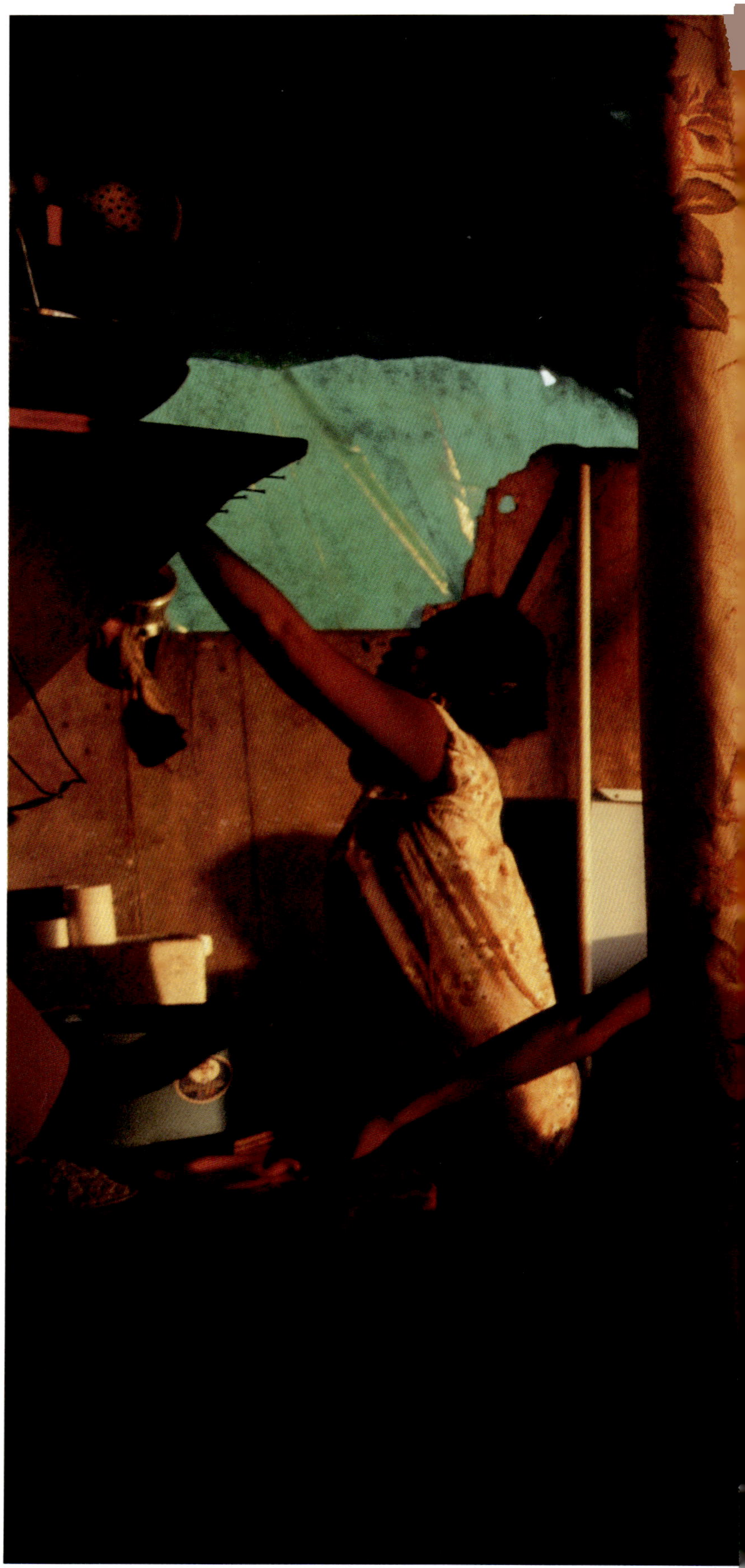

Miguel Rio Branco, *Cortina amarilla* (Yellow curtain), Salvador, Bahia, Brazil, 1984

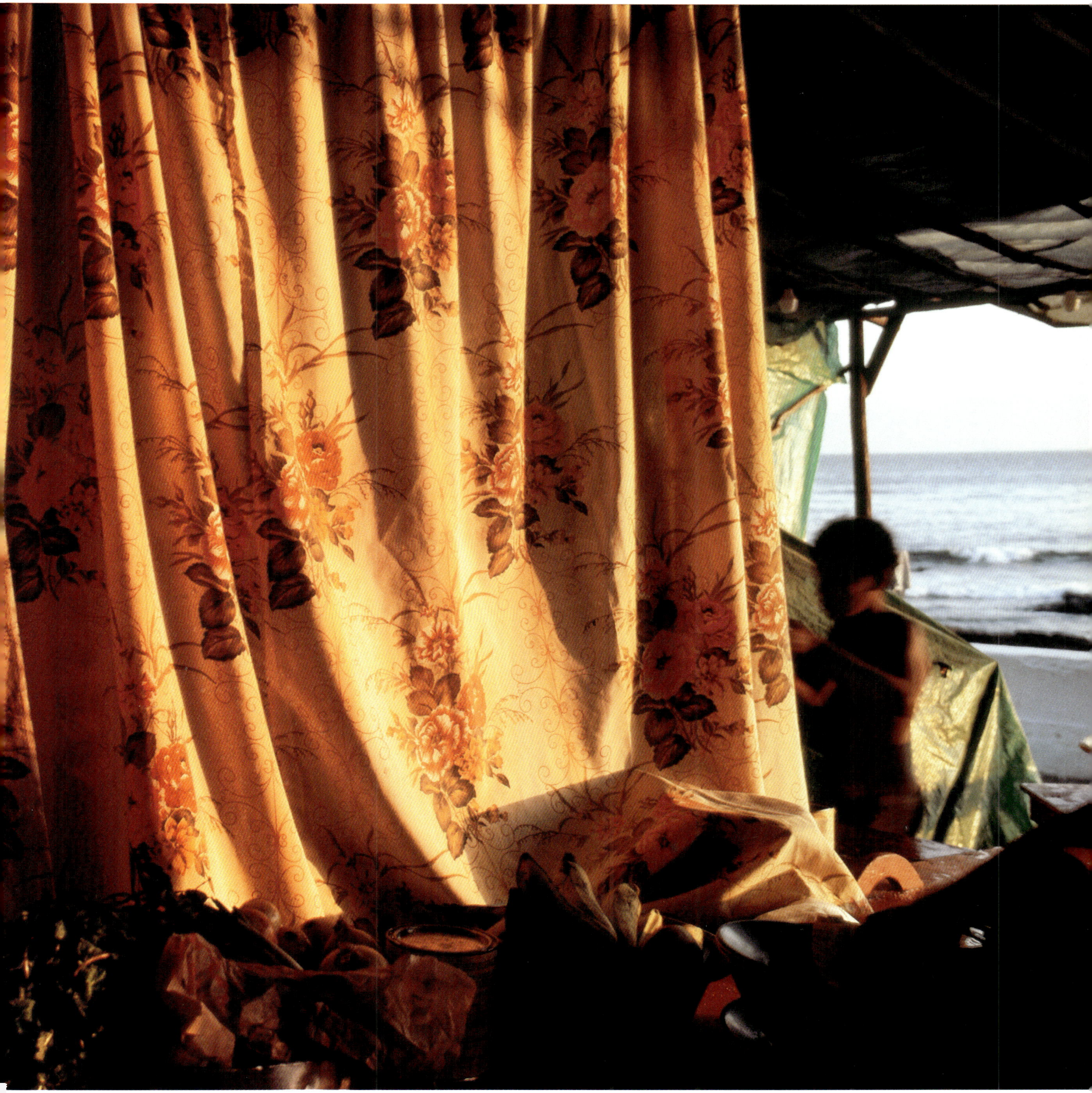

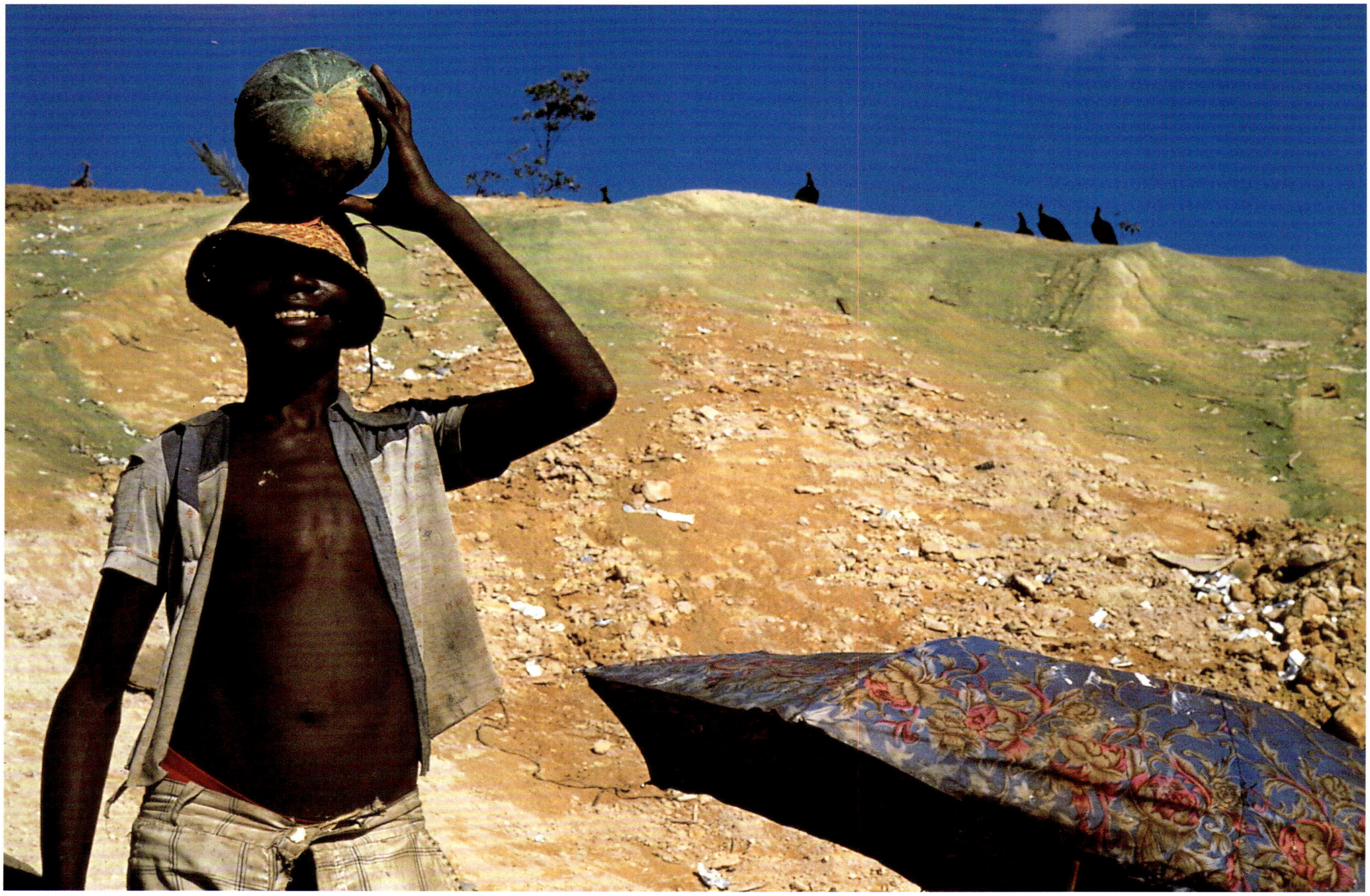

Miguel Rio Branco, *Melancia* (Watermelon), Salvador, Bahia, Brazil, 1985

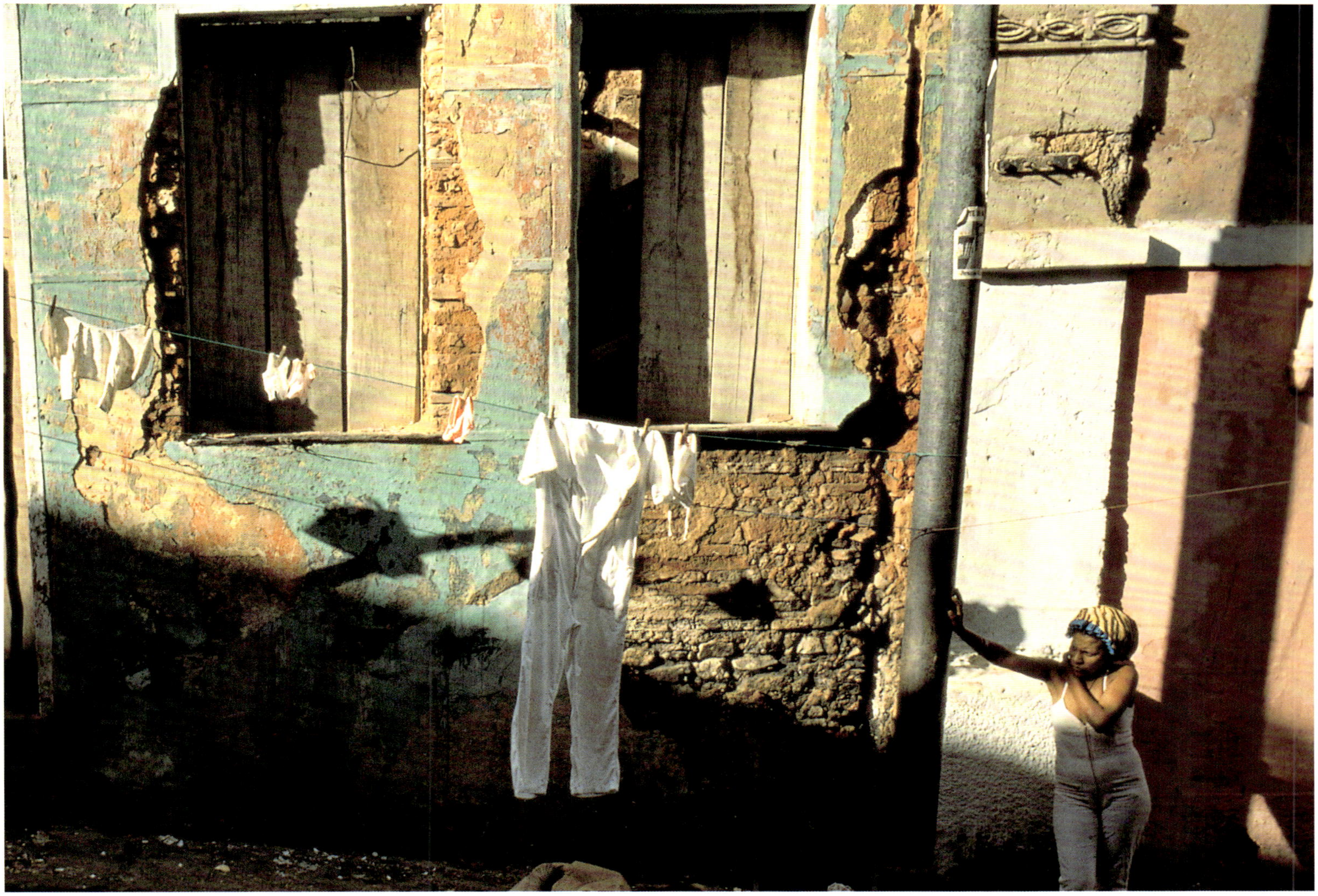

Miguel Rio Branco, *Waiting for the man*, Maciel, Salvador, Bahia, Brazil, 1979

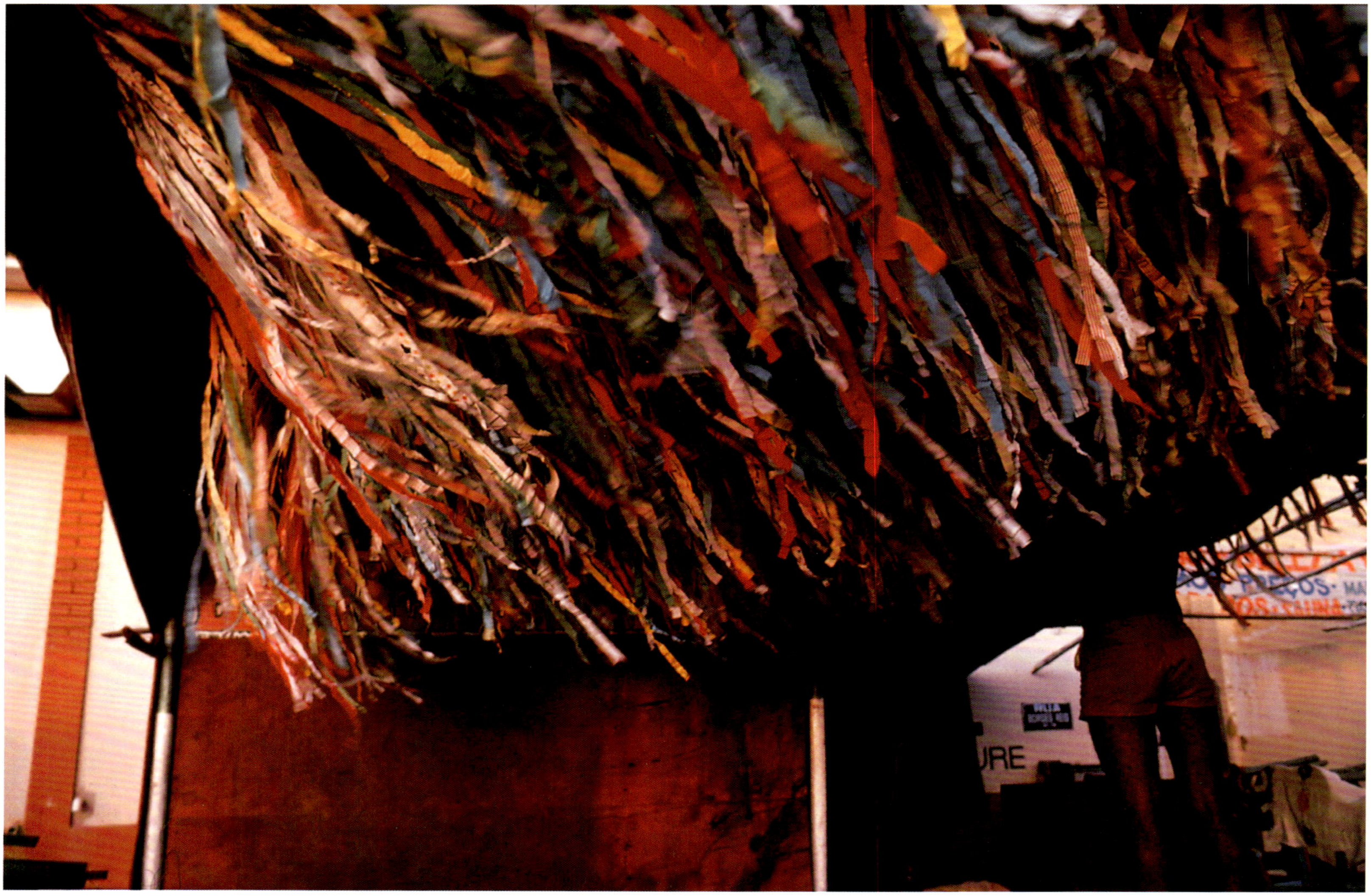

Miguel Rio Branco, *Iemanja Festival*, Rio Vermelho, Salvador, Bahia, Brazil, 1984

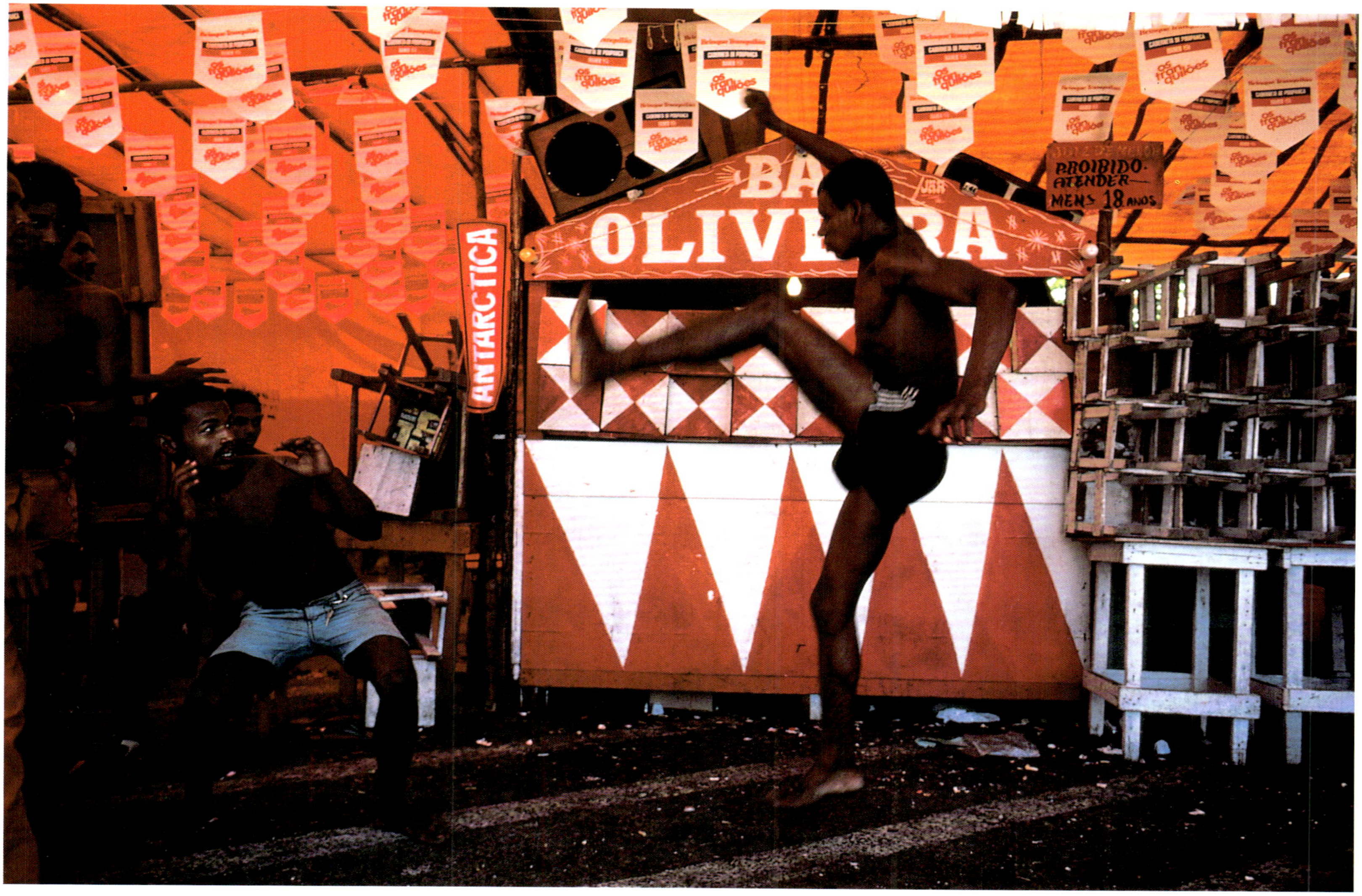


Miguel Rio Branco, *Capoeira*, Salvador, Bahia, Brazil, 1984

er in with the pull of this gravity, these images reveal the common realities of Salvador, but in ways that are more complex than the customary language used to describe them.

Many of the pictures explore the razor's edge between allure and repulsiveness—like discovering scars on a lover's body, especially in a group of images around the Pelourinho district of Salvador. In addition to street vendors, vagrants, and gamblers, this architectural complex is also home to prostitutes, so many of whom are scarred. It remains ambiguous, however, whether their wounds were inflicted by clients or by themselves. A woman clad only in pink underwear is seated on a bed writhing her arms as though she is attempting to fly, in a terrible and moving evocation of a desire for deliverance. Her spread legs are swollen and scarred on account of a medical condition. The image is a visceral study of pleasure and pain, and the elements in the power relations intimately tied to the body as a desired good—perhaps all the more so because it is perishable.

The appealing figure of a nude woman in high heels seen in profile through a doorway suggests another kind of relation whereby mulatas (light-skinned female Afro-Brazilians) are, to quote writer Alma Guillermoprieto, positioned as "glorified sex fetishes," as well as "tribute and proof of the white male's power: his sexual power, and his economic power, which allowed him to wrest the mulata's black mother from her black partner." Likewise, the mulata has served "to perpetuate one of the myths that Brazilians hold most dear, that there is no racism in Brazil, that miscegenation has been natural and pleasant. . . ." In this image, however, Rio Branco challenges a general desire to possess our constructed icons by looking at them: he allows the out-of-focus turn of the subject's unperturbed smile to intensify the viewer's blunt awareness of our own curiosity, pleasure, and intrusion—as set off by bold planes of red against yellow.

Rio Branco has called his photographs "monochromatic variations." The painterly aspect of his work is achieved by using the soft edges caused by movement to produce the quality of a brushstroke, as well as by employing heavy diagonal lines of composition, and by stressing the crossroads of color and plane. A photographer and painter, Rio Branco manipulates those cloudy areas between the "truthfulness" of photography, the classic themes of art history, the happenstance of the snapshot, and the meaningful patterns of the canvas.

One might even suggest that the swells from blue to red or from green to orange enact a structural motion of recession and advancement both formally and thematically: a veritable choreography of ebb and flow, departure and return, a crepuscular passage from twilight to sundown, or from childhood to adolescence to adulthood. Then there are the tonal subtleties between the masculine and feminine, the spectrum of skin. In this, the photographs depict couples and lone figures engaged in seaside or urban exchange, or directly confronting the photographer. (Many images show subjects shielding their faces from the camera, or in an attempt to obstruct the lens.) These images are also about the peripatetic, about walking as crucial to the itinerant ways we see—in compositions taken straight-on or aimed from eye down to ground level, along the sea, through the streets, and back again.

The juxtaposition of images here creates elliptical statements, or intricate relationships between tone and subject. The resulting clash and synthesis richly reverberates with meaning. On the left we see a man carrying a watermelon above his head at the foot of a hill, next to a floral-motif umbrella that fills the bottom right corner. On the right we see a broken-down exterior with two boarded windows, laundry out front, and a woman leaning against a post at bottom right. The clumps of dirt and green deposits along the hill in the first picture echo the exposed bricks and faded plaster of the weathered facade. The gesture and expression of the two human figures forge a statement about the scarcity of means and the inescapable presence of the sun—while several vultures, barely visible behind the hill, render more ominous the disembodied overalls on the facing page.

The title *Dulce sudor amargo* speaks of bittersweet longing, the dubious nature of modifiers as the bitter cancels out the sweet, and the more lasting and palpable reality of sweat by way of toil, pleasure, and place. The book's epigram from Goethe, "Color is the expression and the suffering of light," points to the broadest meaning of these photographs in terms of form and content: they signal the illusory gap that separates the physics of refracted light from the imperative of what an image can and will communicate.

Also a cinematographer, Miguel Rio Branco creates compelling images packed with shadow-lilt and dramatic density. The static or suspended moment is interrupted by some sort of formal strain, our focus deflected for a moment before it can finally concentrate on the totality of the composition—as if mirroring history itself—in gleam and after-image, in bleed and blur. Rio Branco has called *Dulce sudor amargo* a "parable of survival in distress; you can apply it anywhere you like in Brazil, even as a metaphor of the country as a whole."

These photographs were produced at a time when Brazil had endured the despotism and oppression sprung from a long series of military dictatorships and a technocratic authoritarian state for long enough. Brazil has traditionally viewed itself as a country of the future, and Brazilians were optimistic in their demands for *abertura* and a civilian presidency—if oblivious, perhaps, to the simulacrum of "democratic change" that now inhibits countries in Latin America and others throughout the world. An image of clothing stranded on a patch of sand along the beach emerges eerily as the pivotal last note in *Dulce sudor amargo*—as though to suggest the contradictions that can coexist between sensual pleasure and material divestment, between emotional abandon and collective determination, between social promise and the potential threat of a whole future being run aground.

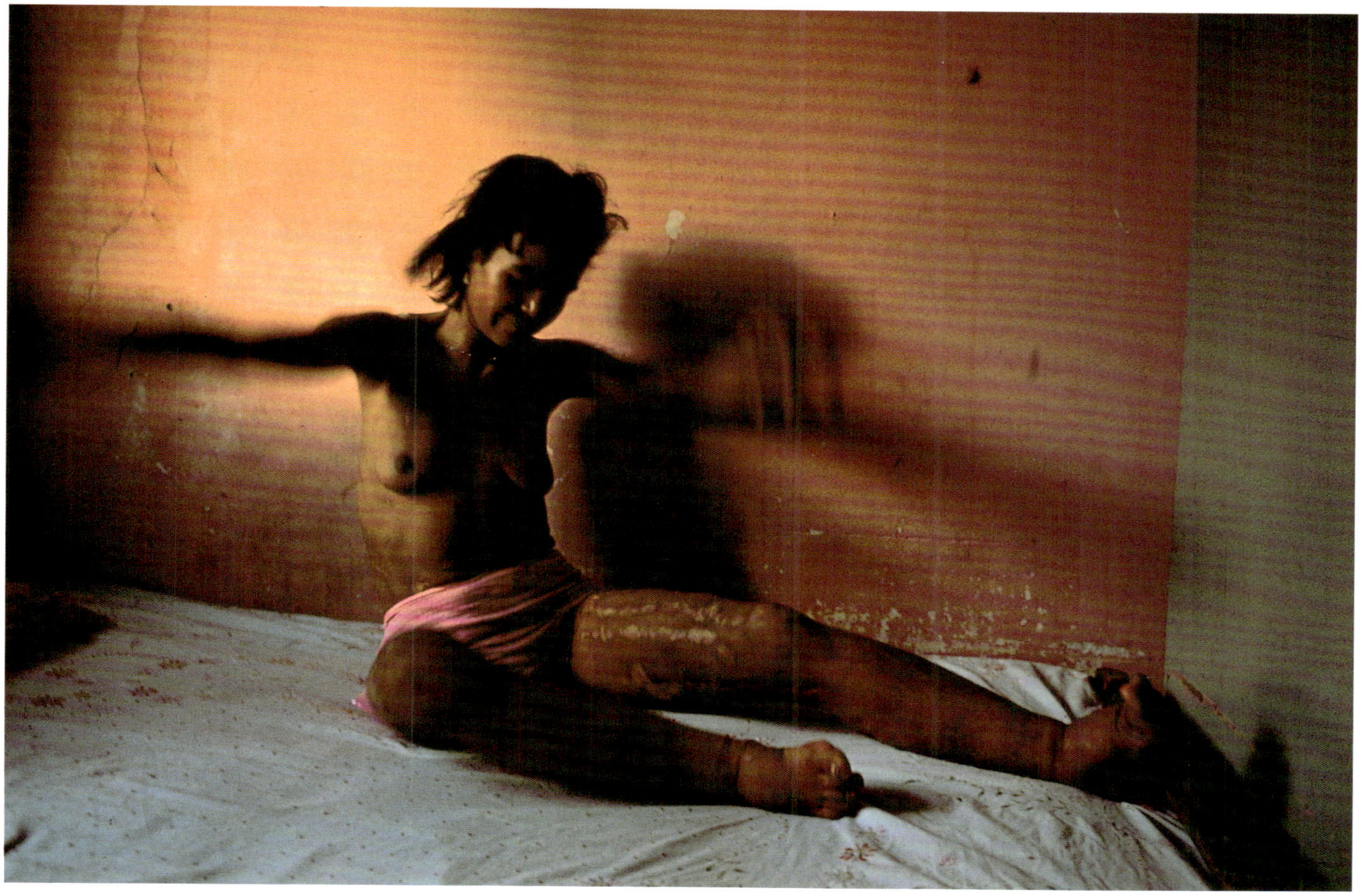

Miguel Rio Branco, *Flying*, Maciel, Salvador, Bahia, Brazil, 1979

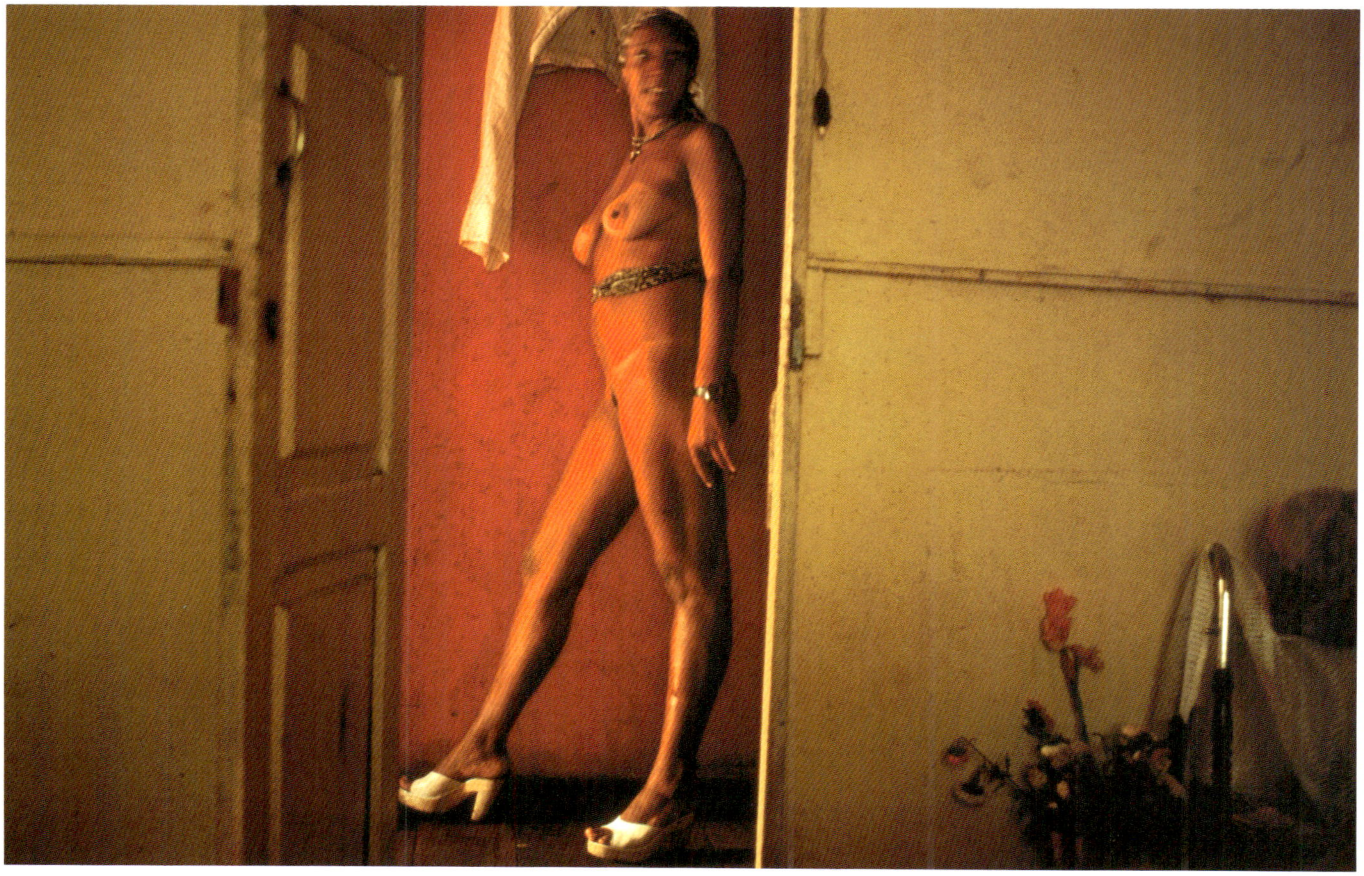

Miguel Rio Branco, *Zapatos blancos* (White shoes), Maciel, Salvador, Bahia, Brazil, 1979

# PEOPLE & IDEAS

## STOWAWAY SUBLIMITY

By Frederick Kaufman

Riding the Rails. *A film by Michael Uys and Lexy Lovell, 1997. Available on video through PBS by telephone (800) 645-4PBS.*

*Riding the Rails* explores a phenomenon that has been too often relegated to the margins of this country's history: how during the Depression an entire generation of adolescents left their homes and families and took to the trains, sleeping in boxcars and in the hobo "jungles" that sprang up outside small towns across America. By the early 1930s, this practice had reached epidemic proportions, as the Southern Pacific Railroad threw more than half a million "hobos" and "vagrants" off their trains. *Riding the Rails* not only salvages images of this scorned tribe, it also salvages their stories. Filmmakers Michael Uys and Lexy Lovell collected more than three thousand letters from survivors of this mass migration. They tracked down individuals who would talk on camera about their transforming experiences, and created a film that is edifying, relevant, touching, and terrifying. Indeed, in its mélange of archival footage, folk songs, photography, and personal witness, *Riding the Rails* captures nothing less than the story of America—a tale of freedom, opportunity, and adventure, and of misery, poverty, and loneliness.

One of this documentary's greatest strengths is that Uys and Lovell do not so much tell this story as allow it to be told. Watching the film is like being in a boxcar at night, a boxcar full of individuals who whisper and shout the secrets of their lives. Thus we meet John Fawcett, a doctor's son, who tells us that he "just ran away from home for adventure" and discovered too late the true wages of wandering: "I was hungry all the time. And I wasn't used to hunger."

We meet René Champion, who quietly informs us that he came from "what would today be called a dysfunctional home." In 1933, at the age of sixteen, Champion left his small town in Pennsylvania. Now in his eighties, the camera tracks him slowly walking along sun-scarred train tracks that lead through a barren landscape. We hear his gripping account of being left on a desert highway more than half a century ago:

> *It's a terribly lonely feeling when you're in the wide open spaces, so beautiful and wonderful during the day. But at night, for miles and miles you see no light. Some of the worst feelings of loneliness that I've ever experienced in my life were in situations like this.*

If Champion's voice emerges here as plain-spoken sublime, it is in great part thanks to Uys and Lovell's editing technique, which is steady, rhythmic, and unflinching. The duo excells in visual and aural montage, and this film offers a number of haunting sequences as darklit trains hurtle into infinite horizons and choruses of "This land was made for you and me" rise up like a dirge.

Champion is today a professor of anthropology; but *Riding the Rails* has room not only for the voices and visages of those who became missionaries, union organizers, and political activists, but also for meatpackers, pipe fitters, and groundskeepers. Uys and Lovell present us with Clarence Lee, whose sharecropper father told him at the height of the Depression that he had to leave home. Lee was sixteen years old at the time.

In a broken voice, Lee recounts that even on the nights when his traveling companions were invited into a house, he had to sleep in the barn with the animals. He tells how he barely escaped lynching by jumping off a midnight train into a Louisiana swamp. And then Uys and Lovell show us faces of suffering and hunger that transcend race and age and gender, devastating images of families and children that literalize the expression "dirt poor."

For hoboing was not strictly a male province. Here is Peggy DuHart, who left her father's Wyoming farm in 1938 at the age of fifteen and with her friend Irene—who was, unbeknownst to DuHart, already three months pregnant—rode the rails west. As she sits on abandoned track amid lush grasses and trees that suggest the endless spring of memory, DuHart reads the letters she wrote home. The white-haired lady talks about the intricacies and dangers of hopping onto trains, about Irene's pregnancy, and about the rodeo riders who invited the two girls to share their pot of beans and their tent somewhere in Idaho. One of these cowboys became Irene's new boyfriend, which was, for DuHart, the final straw. DuHart tells how she finally found the courage to steal onto a train by herself heading back "across the mountains," and how she made it home "in time for supper" and was welcomed, not scolded. "But it was still hard times."

Hard times, indeed: "We went from middle class gentility to scrabble-ass poor overnight," recalls Bob "Guitar Whitey" Symmonds. When his father's security business went belly-up in 1938, he took to the rails. "You ride a freight train one time, and you're hooked." And hooked he remains. Now retired, "Guitar Whitey" not only performs a good portion of this film's soundtrack, he still averages about 2,500 miles a year on freight trains.

Of course, Uys and Lovell cannot resist the temptation to hop on board with Symmonds, and some of the film's most intriguing footage ensues, as the housing tracts and fields of Mexican migrant workers that mark the Pacific coast today seamlessly blend into archival images of a black-and-white California that seemed nothing less than paradise. For a moment, past and present merge into a single vision, a single sea. And then we, like Depression-era riders themselves, are brought back to the harsh reality: in 1936, Los Angeles authorities, panicking about the number of homeless people flooding their city, blockaded California's eastern border. Abused by club-wielding detectives, rounded up, strip-searched,

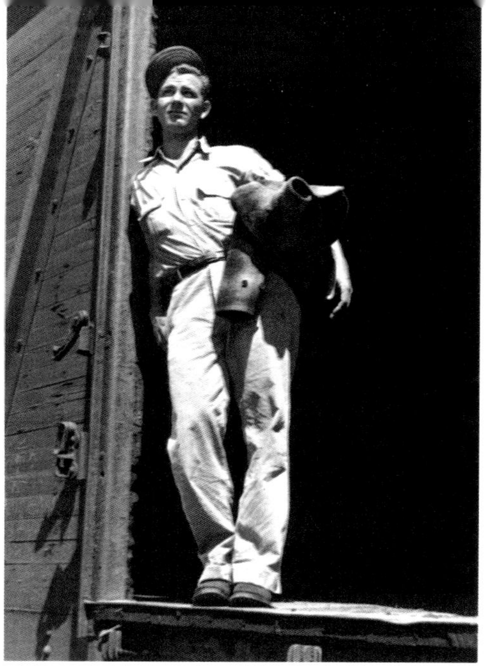

driven out, and left with nothing but coal-stained phlegm as a souvenir, the youth of America soon learned the sad truth about the West and its promises:

*. . . believe it or not,*
*You won't find it so hot,*
*If you ain't got the do re mi . . .*

Uys and Lovell do not leave us in despair. The final images of the film depict America rising out of the Depression, and show how many of the young men and women who had found themselves reduced to beggary were finally able to make a decent living by signing on with New Deal agencies like the Citizens Conservation Corps. On the other hand, Uys and Lovell do not shy away from a clear-eyed appraisal of the damage done. While the implications of extreme psychic loss never remain far from the surface, the filmmakers refuse to preach and their film is, to its immense credit, utterly lacking in didacticism.

In one way or another, *Riding the Rails* touches all of us. Many years ago my grandfather and namesake, Frederick Kaufman, after an adolescence spent driving cattle up and down Idaho's Coeur d'Alene, rode the rails home to Baltimore. When he finally tumbled off the train, what he needed was a drink. He repaired to the nearest bar. And it was there that he met the father of the woman who would eventually become his wife. After regaling this stranger with tales of his cowboy life and of his long journey home in open-air boxcars, he was granted an invitation to dinner.

And the rest, as they say, is history.

## LETTERS TO THE EDITOR

*Charles Bowden gave a speech entitled "Blind in the Sun" in June of 1997 at the Center for Creative Photography in Tucson, Arizona, discussing his thoughts on desert photography. We featured his talk in the People & Ideas section of* Aperture *#150, "Moments of Grace." It elicited a strong response from numerous readers, prompting us to run a Letters to the Editor column.*

*From Thomas Wiewandt:*

### GONE CRAZY IN THE SUN

In March, a friend and colleague from back East sent me a copy of the essay "Blind in the Sun," written by Charles Bowden and published in your 1998 Winter issue (pp. 74–76). His letter said, "Enclosed is an article on desert photography (I think) from *Aperture* magazine. I've got mixed feelings about it; perhaps Charles should be congratulated and chump-slapped for his little ditty. Let me know." For a Tucsonan, it might be easy to shirk this one off; but knowing that many of your readers have never experienced the desert Southwest or Bowden's shoot-from-the-hip brand of journalism, which in this case was more of a miss than a hit, I feel obligated to respond.

Having read Charles Bowden's description of his attempt to cross the Camino del Diablo on foot, Nancy Solomon of the Center for Creative Photography invited him to speak at the opening of Lee Friedlander's summer show, which featured a body of work that was made to emphasize a harsh desert landscape viewed from the interior of every tangled bush on the face of our land. Like it or not, Friedlander's take on this environment is different—not the sort of thing most people would want hanging on the living room wall. But the words, as delivered by Bowden, say more about the writer than the show. He evidently sees the desert as a resilient, indifferent land with no soul . . . an intolerably hot, colorless place flattened by blinding white light . . . a monotonous expanse with no focal points . . . "a messy living thing." And those of us photographers, writers, filmmakers, or artists who don't believe this and portray it otherwise are said to be members of a cult shut-off from real-life experiences.

To be kind, I would suggest that Bowden's ill-fated trek on the Camino del Diablo has left *him* blinded by the sun. For anyone to attempt such a crossing, unprepared, walking in the heat of midday, in midsummer, is just plain stupid. And could this coffee fanatic be unaware that caffeine closes down peripheral circulation, limiting our ability to lose heat through the skin? At first, I thought this to be tongue-in-cheek humor, but after reading on, I'm not so sure anymore. Perhaps next time he should try this crossing in a suit of armor or, better yet, stark naked. And what about the buddy who he left behind in the dust when the going got disastrously rough? Think nothing of it, folks . . . just getting a real-life experience in the desert to write about. With friends like this, who needs enemies!

Bowden's piece is jammed with half-truths. I agree that certain points of view have become overworked and tiresome in photography as in most other forms of expression, but this is certainly not characteristic of or limited to deserts. Editorial biases of publishers are strong; each develops a market and "look" aimed at economic success. And what readers want is not always in the best interests of us photographers; unfortunately, conformity rules. And publishers are quick to copy the economic successes of others, fostering more conformity. Conversely, as a writer, Bowden seems to be aiming for recognition through nonconformity, even at the expense of saying something meaningful. I hope that *Aperture* paid him no more for his peculiar point of view than I'm being compensated for this response.

That said, I'd like to address Bowden's ten "rock-hard truths" about desert photography, some of which overlap and have been summarized as seven points here:

1. *Desert photography insists the desert is fragile*, a view that Bowden can't comprehend. The concept of fragility has nothing to do with the fact that deserts are on the march worldwide, stemming from our abuse of nondesert lands. Truth is, abandoned wagon trails from the last

century are still clearly visible in desert regions; and in southern California, ORVs (off-road vehicles) have completely stripped the land of vegetation in some places and have left a maze of scars on the land elsewhere, even in parks where there is insufficient manpower to regulate vehicle access. If all cross-country traffic were to cease tomorrow, the wounds would never heal over in our lifetimes. Because desert lands receive little rainfall, shrubs and trees grow slowly, and few prosper in finely compacted soil. When rains do come, they are often violent, which leads to erosion and loss of soil. In the Great Basin Desert of northern Arizona and Utah, the soil is stabilized by a delicate crust of cryptogams—lichen, moss, algae, and fungi—a living crust that is easily broken by hikers. Once damaged, the crust requires decades to recover. To say or imply that deserts are fragile is more than justified by the facts.

2. *Desert photography can contain no signs of humankind.* Partially true. I would guess that most of us "cult" members who have made innumerable sacrifices to succeed as nature photographers entered the profession because we are spiritually moved by places that at least feel untouched by the hand of man. Raw wilderness is becoming so rare that it's now a challenge to capture a scene void of power lines, contrails, road cuts, bottles, graffiti, etc., especially in deserts, where artifacts are seldom hidden from view. So we work harder and venture farther to escape civilization and to capture on film what we love the most. Likewise, readers/viewers want to be transported there vicariously, into mysterious and beautiful places, a demand that feeds an enormous publishing industry hungry for images that just might rekindle that sense of wonder in us all and strengthen our connections with a natural world that needs our help.

On the flip side, many of us document or create art from the most graphic examples of destruction we see in our travels, be it a forest clear-cut, an oil-covered beach, or vehicular scars on the desert's face. Publishers rarely ask for such material, so most such images remain hidden from public view.

3. *The only focal point in the desert exists in desert photography.* Such words could only be spoken by a person with unfocused, scattered perceptions, perhaps the unfortunate consequence of having one's brains fried in the sun. This statement seems to have come from a jaded reporter playing into the all-too-common notion that deserts are uniform and monotonous, barren wastes of little visual interest. Perhaps what Bowden calls "desert egotists"—mountains, cacti, birds, serpents, etc.—are unworthy of his undivided attention. Problem is, Bowden's ego is so big that he can't see beyond it. Something as "insignificant" as the curve of a cactus spine can be inspiring, whether photographed or not.

4. *Desert photography has no white light and a taboo against heat and thirst.* Bowden evidently believes that to have a real-life experience in the desert, one must confront the elements head-on, at high noon in midsummer, as he so foolishly did on the Camino del Diablo. Yet he points out that virtually every living creature is adapted to *avoid* these extremes—could it be that *he* is the one who is out of step with reality?!? The very concept of a siesta pays allegiance to desert heat, the time to lay low.

Most photographers choose to photograph the desert at more hospitable times, at times when the desert comes to life, biologically and aesthetically. Nothing can compare with the fervor for life that's evident during the cooler hours of day and through the night, especially after a rainstorm. And to experience those rare and fleeting episodes of a desert wildflower bloom, like the one that graced the Southwest this year, is to witness one of the greatest evolutionary achievements on Earth. Imagine a gazillion seeds lying dormant for a quarter of a century just waiting for that one moment in time when all conditions are right for an orgasmic explosion, all in the name of survival. It's certainly no wonder that there's a stampede of photographers on such occasions. For those of us in the "cult" who join in this jubilation, are we "willfully blind" and "protected from experience"? I think not.

Incidentally, Bowden is not the first to liken nature photographers to pornographers, a concept that rubs me the wrong way, but the least he can do is give credit to the writer who came up with the idea: José Knighton, manager of the Back of Beyond bookstore in Moab, Utah.

5. *Desert photography has a prurient interest in reds, oranges, and Fuji blues.* The desert Southwest offers an elusive palette that is not only astonishing but truly unbelievable, a phantasmagoria of colors that will blow most people's minds. Overall, it goes unrivaled in North America, save the outrageous hues that often touch the autumn landscape of New England. In early morning and late afternoon hours, red light predominates, the closer to sunset the redder the light, a physical phenomenon that we all know well. Red light adds drama to the landscape, drama that is exaggerated by some films, imparting a hellfire-and-brimstone look to the subject unless held back with a blue-tinted filter. But here's another fact of life: red sells, and editors seldom steer away from images of mountains lit by the setting sun or sandstone monoliths infused with iron oxide. So intentional or not, red desert landscapes are here to stay. Regarding "Fuji blues," Bowden might be referring to one popular film, Velvia, noted for its saturated colors; or perhaps he's confusing films with the effect of a polarizer.

In the real world, color separations and printing also determine what the public sees. Although interested in color photography, Ansel Adams steered away from it because the image-maker has so little control over color that reaches the printed page. Scan some old art books and magazines to see how much color printing has improved during the past thirty years; although astonishingly better, quality remains inconsistent and still falls short of what most photographers would like to see.

6. *Desert photography believes the dry ground is an aesthetic experience and not a messy, living thing.* This is a tough one to swallow, knowing that Bowden has traversed Baja California and the lava fields straddling the Mexican-American border from Organ Pipe Cactus National Monument to the Pinacate biosphere reserve. Much of this region appears to have been planted with the care and precision of a Japanese garden. Although seldom photographed, even the creosote bush flats illustrate remarkable order and uniformity in design. Strong images of anything on this planet usually come from

graphic simplicity, and deserts offer a perfect milieu for the creation of photographic art. If chaos is there, it lies in the eye of the beholder.

7. *Desert photography assumes that these are sacred places, ancient and polluted with wisdom.* Simply put, deserts have inspired countless pioneers, artists, and writers over the ages, some no doubt moved to tears by the majesty found here. What's the point in raining on their parade?

I have one last bone to pick with Bowden's report: his slipshod little story about Bryce Canyon National Park. In his words, "1.6 million people visit Bryce each year. . . . Of the 1.6 million visitors, three hundred . . . ask for a permit so that they can get out of their cars and walk away from the road." Truth is, the Bryce Canyon amphitheater is honeycombed with thirty-five miles of hiking trails for daytime use, none of which requires a backcountry permit—in fact, the most spectacular "hoodoos" (colorful eroded landforms) that have made Bryce so famous lie not in the backcountry but along the trails that descend into the canyon. One of the most popular trails is a fairly strenuous (521-ft. descent/ascent), three-mile loop from Sunset Point to Sunrise Point. When it's not treacherously covered in mud, snow, or ice, hundreds of visitors hike this trail *daily*.

Tucson offers a rich and varied community of artistic talent, which makes Bowden's remarks all the more offensive. For a look at what many contemporary desert photographers are up to, I recommend that he look beyond the pages of *Arizona Highways*, attend more of our local photographic exhibits, and visit Swanstock, a Tucson-based agency (now an affiliate of The Image Bank) that specializes in photographic art. And any writer who wants to get in touch with what nature photographers really think, feel, and strive for should attend the annual forum of the North American Nature Photographers Association. Membership is open to writers, publishers, and educators, as well as photographers [visit our web page at http://www.mcs.net/rjacobs/nanpa.htm; or ask for membership information via e-mail, nanpa@resourcenter.com, or by calling (303) 422-8527].

I was obviously infuriated that the editors at *Aperture* saw fit to publish Bowden's essay; he's certainly no art critic and clearly knows nothing about photography. Having read some of his other work, this piece seems intentionally antagonistic, an attempt to get noticed. Times must be rough, Chuck, when bad publicity is better than no publicity. Let's all put this one quietly to bed.

*Thomas Wiewandt is a freelance nature photographer and owner of Wild Horizons, a business devoted to independent publishing and instructional photographic safaris. He's the author of* Hidden Life of the Desert *(Crown/Random House), has made three award-winning films for the National Geographic Society, and has had work featured in* National Wildlife, Smithsonian, GEO, OMNI, Audubon, *and* Arizona Highways, *among others.*

*From Diana Kappel-Smith:*

Dear *Aperture* (and Chuck Bowden):

Reading Bowden's "Blind in the Sun" has left me nearly incoherent with rage; it has taken me some weeks to calm down enough to attempt a reply. Maybe this was Mr. Bowden's purpose—to insult the intelligence of those photographers and writers and poets and painters ("daubers"? Please!) and—who knows?—musicians, dramatists, shamans, prophets, *et al*, who have found deserts to be the locus of inspiration.

There's so much wrong-headed and plain *wrong* in his speech/essay that I don't know where to begin. . . . Well, let's go right to Mr. Bowden's Ten Commandments of Desert Photography. Like the original Commandments, these are a codification of what has been obvious for years; but unlike those others, his are couched in a language fuming with crabbiness. And his goal is not to enlighten or instruct, but to condemn. (Now, having received these truths, Chuck, are we meant to consider you the Moses of Modern Media? And we're supposed to follow you to . . . say again?) These commandments—though they make some telling points—mostly reveal Mr. Bowden's ignorance.

Let me choose one of these that I know something about: the one where he states that being a desert photographer is not a full-time job. The photogs he knows apparently hop from their Toyotas any old place to snatch that "magic moment" before they go back to holding down a barstool. Well, I've had the honor of working and traveling in the deserts of Africa and North America with lots of photographers, some of the best in the world, for weeks on end sometimes. And I can promise you that they put in fourteen hour days at a minimum, and they regularly make treks that make Mr. Bowden's *journada de muerto* hoo-rah look like a trot to the mailbox.

Then there's the one where Mr. Bowden states that "Desert photography has a prurient interest in reds, oranges, and Fuji blues. It is a place of colors I have seldom seen this side of my acid trips." Oh boy. I'm sorry that his fixations with life-threatening bright-light experience and acidic nerve-fusion have prevented him from, well, not just seeing those colors out there but being *soaked* in them, bathed in a Color Experience that no photographer *can* capture; though, thank God, the good ones are driven to try. Color is what desert *does*. And it's brief and—yes—orgasmic. (Is there something *wrong* with this? Chuck, even cacti, snakes, and ephemeral flowers do their color for good reasons; sex or power mostly. On the other hand, the sun and atmosphere and mountains and playas do it for no reason other than obeisance to the laws of physics. And they routinely blow one's socks off. Visual artists respond to this even if you can't. And visual artists are *supposed to try to blow our socks off* by whatever means they can—True Colors be damned! Try talking your prurient color nonsense to a Basquiat or Rothko! OK, so they're not with us anymore. But if they were, would you *dare* to say it to them? OK, so why say such nonsense to anyone?)

As to the lengthy condemnation of "Virtual Nature" freaks: Hey, Chuck, this is not news. Twenty-five years ago the statistics said that only one-half of one percent of visitors to national parks went more than one hundred yards from their vehicles. Those numbers haven't changed. So, most people *are* content to experience the gritty world from a distance. Which is the only reason there's still some gritty wild world out there for those crazies among us to actually *be* in. I've always thought this was a good thing.

Exaggerated images of nature have a long human history, a fact that Mr. Bowden seems to have ignored. "Virtual" as they are, the Lascaux cave paintings and Cablevision's *Animal Planet* have more in common than we admit. Though the sacred images have changed, they're no less powerful for being conveyed by different means.

Due to the efforts of nature photographers, filmmakers, writers, poets, painters—cliché-ridden and commerce-driven as their efforts may sometimes be—environmental awareness in this country is at an all-time high. Eighty-three percent of the populace believes that environmental quality and wilderness conservation should be *the* top national priorities. Where do we think this belief came from? It came from what writers and photographers feel, respond to, express, and publish. It comes from what they *see.*

Too bad that all Mr. Bowden sees when he's out there is a "mirror." Given the tenor of his essay, this bit of narcissism doesn't surprise me. But it is disappointing.

Hey, so maybe Mr. Bowden was just trying to be provocative. And I like provocative—that's part of any artist's job, perhaps the most important part. Any good artist prods the conscience, pokes sacred cows, blasts the profane, reveals the sacred, *provokes*—all with the goal of opening eyes to truths they may not have seen or wanted to see. But in this case I believe that Mr. Bowden was insulting desert photography—and photographers—simply to swell his own ego. He was behaving like an unhappy child who smashes things just to get attention. I've been an admirer of Chuck Bowden's work for years, but after "Blind in the Sun" I can no longer trust him. Having set out—I believe, I hope—with the laudable task of steering desert photography away from cliché and toward some deeper attention, he has revealed himself to be the worst cliché of all: the egocentric blowhard who can't be bothered to get his facts straight.

*Diana Kappel-Smith is the author of three books of nature writing, including* Desert Time, *now in paperback from University of Arizona Press. Her essays on desert subjects have appeared in* Smithsonian, Orion *magazine, and* Best American Essays.

## CONTRIBUTORS

VÍCTOR FLORES OLEA has served as a diplomat, Secretary of Culture of the Mexican Government, and Ambassador at the United Nations (1994). He is the author of three photography books. Presently he is a researcher and writer of political editorials in Mexico.

JOAN FONTCUBERTA has a long history in photography as an artist, professor, and writer. In the U.S., his work is shown regularly by Zabriskie Gallery in New York. He has recently authored two collections of essays: *El beso de Judas: Fotografía y verdad* (1997), and *Ciencia y fricción* (1998).

ALMA GUILLERMOPRIETO is a Mexican journalist who has been writing about Latin America for twenty years. She is the author of two books: *Samba* (1990), and *The Heart That Bleeds: Latin America Now* (1995).

FREDERICK KAUFMAN's writing has appeared in the *New York Times Magazine*, the *Village Voice Literary Supplement*, *Gentlemen's Quarterly*, and numerous other publications. His most recent book is *Manuel Álvarez Bravo: Photographs and Memories* (1997).

CARLOS MONSIVÁIS was born in Mexico in 1938. His work as a writer, journalist, and anthologist includes: *Escenas de pudor y liviandad* (1978), *Nuevo catecismo para indios remisos* (1982), *Entrada libre: Crónicas de la sociedad que se organiza* (1988), *Los mil y un velorios* (1994), *Los rituales del caos* (1995), and *Mexican Postcards* (1997).

ÁLVARO MUTIS was born in Bogotá, Colombia and has lived in Mexico since 1956. His first poetry was published in 1948, his first short stories in 1978, and his first novella in 1986. He has received various literary awards, and his poetry has appeared in *The New Yorker*. Three of his novellas have been published in a single volume entitled *Maqroll* (1992).

PABLO ORTIZ MONASTERIO was born in Mexico City in 1952. He has edited and managed three significant projects: *México indígena* (seven titles), *Río de Luz* (twenty titles), and *Luna Córnea* at Centro de la Imagen (a quarterly periodical). He is the cofounder of Consejo Mexicano de Fotografía and founder of Centro de la Imagen. A widely exhibited and collected photographer, the most recent publication of his work is *The Last City/La última ciudad* (1995).

ROBERTO TEJADA is a poet and writer on the arts. He has lived in Mexico City where he was on the editorial staff of *Vuelta* magazine, and later served as executive editor of *Artes de México*. He is currently assistant curator of the Wittliff Gallery of Southwestern & Mexican Photography housed at Southwest Texas State University in San Marcos.

RAQUEL TIBOL was born in Argentina in 1923 and has spent most of her professional career as writer, art critic, and journalist in Mexico. Since 1976 she has published the weekly column "Arte" in the magazine *Proceso*. She has worked internationally as a curator and lecturer, and has published over thirty books.

VERÓNICA VOLKOW has published five books of poetry, most recently *Arcanos* (1996) and *Colección práctica mortal*. She is also author of *Sudáfrica: Diario de un viaje* (1988), an account of daily life under apartheid, and *La mordedura de la risa: Un estudio sobre la obra gráfica de Francisco Toledo en México* (1995).

## CREDITS

Unless otherwise noted, all photographs and texts are courtesy of and copyright by the artists. Pp. 13–17 © Fototeca del INAH, Mexico, Fondo Casasola; pp. 27–31 © Fundació Renau, Valencia, Spain; pp. 41, 44–45 © Fototeca del INAH, Mexico, Fondo Nacho López; pp. 50–51 © Abbas/Magnum Photos, Inc., NY; p. 63 © Fototeca del INAH, Mexico, donation Carlos Vidali; p. 77 courtesy of the National Archives.

"Josep Renau: 'The American Way of Life'" is a revised version of the original Spanish. "Josep Renau: Fotomontador" and "Historia Natural de las Cosas" were published in the original Río de Luz books of those titles.

Some caption translations by Cola Franzen.